I Don't Buy Green Bananas

(center stage with cancer)

Hilary,
Thank you for
years of Christian
fellowship.
Joanie B.

Joanie Butman

iUniverse, Inc.

New York Bloomington

I Don't Buy Green Bananas
(center stage with cancer)

iUniverse books may be ordered through booksellers or by contacting:

iUniverse
1663 Liberty Drive
Bloomington, IN 47403
www.iuniverse.com
1-800-Authors (1-800-288-4677)

Because of the dynamic nature of the Internet, any Web addresses or links contained in this book may have changed since publication and may no longer be valid.

ISBN: 978-1-4502-0624-2 (pbk)
ISBN: 978-1-4502-0625-9 (ebk)

Printed in the United States of America

iUniverse rev. date: 2/5/2010

I love to tell the story of unseen things above.
Of Jesus and His glory,
of Jesus and His love.
I love to tell the story,
it did so much for me;
And that is just the reason I tell it now to thee.

Author Unknown

Dedicated to all the health care workers and professionals who choose to walk beside those of us who find ourselves on this difficult journey. And especially to those who still remember why they chose this path, and honor that decision by sprinkling it with a healthy dose of kindness and compassion. I would also like to include my fellow travelers who have been an invaluable source of empathy, support, and encouragement. In their honor, I now pay it forward in the hope that someone will receive the same benefit from this book.

Acknowledgments

For once, I am at a loss for words. There are none adequate enough to express the gratitude I feel for the loving care my husband has bestowed on me, not just this year but for the past nineteen years. He has more than honored his vow to love and to cherish, in sickness and in health. Your gift, my love, is nurturing (among many others). Thanks to my children who continue to bring joy to my days and laundry to my office. Always, and in all ways, I remain indebted to my parents for never giving up on me. And last, but certainly not least, my appreciation to my sister, Terrianne Meier, my sister-in-law, Donna Maresca, and my friends, Todd Baker and Lisa Clarke, for their editorial corrections, comments, and contributions.

Contents

Introduction

On Friday, December 14, 2007 I attended a talk by Kathy Keller at a friend's house with no suspicion that I was walking into a God moment. In fact, I thought I was going to listen to her husband, Rev. Tim Keller, Pastor of Redeemer Presbyterian Church in New York City. It appears that Mrs. Keller had something to say that God thought was more important. As it turned out, her topic was suffering, which proved to be prophetic in its timing. Just four days later, I learned there was a large, malignant tumor residing in my belly. One of her points that stuck with me was the importance of testifying to what God has brought you through to inspire others. She considers it a waste of time and tears if you don't use your experiences to encourage others – something she calls "meaningless sorrow."

It is because of her words that I chose to document my journey, which is unremarkable compared to so many other cancer patients. It is my hope that someone may find comfort in my story. You will notice that I repeat many of the same verses throughout. It is not for lack of imagination or material, but these are the scriptures I return to time and again for comfort and courage. I encourage you to build your own arsenal of favorite scriptures from which you can draw strength, assurance, and peace – ones that will live in your heart and pop into your mind automatically in times of distress rather than fear and anxiety.

One last note, this book is not meant to be a literary masterpiece but a diary of the crazy things that run through one's mind following a cancer diagnosis. I considered calling it *Oh, The Things You Think!* but discovered Dr. Seuss already claimed a similar title. Jokingly, I thought of the 1970's movie, *Diary of a Mad Housewife.* I certainly fit that description before *and* after my diagnosis. Regardless of what it's called, it is merely a reflection of my intimate meeting with cancer and the lessons I learned from the experience. I write it full of gratitude to the doctors and scientists who have brought us to a time when a cancer diagnosis doesn't necessarily arrive with a death sentence. Yes, cancer and I can coexist. It's just up to God to determine how long.

The Road to Calgary

Carrying his own cross,
he went out to the place of the Skull.
Here they crucified him,
and with him two others—
one on each side and Jesus in the middle.
John 19:17-18

Whenever I claim not to be a writer, I am not kidding nor is it false modesty. In fact, I am sure there are a slew of people out there who would agree wholeheartedly. Either way, my disclaimer is a simple fact. There is no better example than my last publishing debacle. But before I begin that story, let me first tell you that for as little as $500 anyone can publish a book. That doesn't mean you are a good writer or that your book is necessarily worth reading, and mine are no exception.

People frequently ask how my books are doing, and sadly I have no answer. Monetarily, no one is ever going to get rich from the sales of my books, even though the beneficiaries could use a financial boost. In case you are unaware, all proceeds from my books go to various non-profit entities. As far as I'm concerned, sales cannot be measured by the funds they generate but by the hearts they reach, and that is not easily tracked. Though I do not realize any monetary gain from writing, the occasional notes and letters I've received from readers who have been affected enough to write them are infinitely more valuable. They are the reason I write. They are an affirmation from God that I understood His instructions. They are also proof that you don't need to be a theologian or an accomplished author to touch people's souls. All any of us can hope to do is reveal how God has worked in our lives, and live in a way that awakens a desire in others to discover Him for themselves.

My most recent foray into the publishing world was like so many of my endeavors – a comedy of errors. After having a number of people edit and proof my draft and correcting the myriad of mistakes they discovered, I sent it off to the publisher. Then, after a number of rounds of proofing and correcting online, I couldn't bear to read it yet again. I agreed it was ready for printing. The day I received the call telling me my author's copy was ready a song came on the radio while I was driving. When you have XM radio, the title of whatever is playing is displayed. I can't recall the song but remember glancing at the screen and seeing the word Calvary in the title. I remember thinking, "That's weird, it's supposed to be Calgary." With an increasing sense of foreboding, it triggered something in my brain and a sinking feeling in my stomach. I could clearly see the sentence in my now published book where I refer to Jesus' walk to Calgary *not* Calvary. Then I thought, "That's nothing. You've misspelled the word acknowledgments in your past three books," but I couldn't deny that this mistake carried a little more significance. I wish I could claim it was a typo, but I have to admit I have always had a mental block about the name, and confuse Calvary and Calgary often. I don't know why – maybe too many hockey games, which would be my only association with Calgary. However, when you say it fast enough, no one notices. I assume that's why no one has ever corrected me. It's not like it comes up often in casual conversation. The few times that it might is usually with those who know what you are talking about, so they hear what they think you *must* be saying.

I immediately dialed the publisher and begged for them to change that one letter. No problem, for $300 we can recall the book and change up to twenty errors. Interesting dilemma. My initial thought was if the five people who read it didn't pick up on it, would anyone else? Maybe if you know what the name is, your mind just slides over it, seeing only what it expects. I made the mistake of telling my parents, whose laughter turned to shock when they realized I was considering leaving the book as is. They were appalled. "What difference does it make?" I asked, not expecting the reaction that comment evoked. My thought was that it was Christ's death and resurrection that saved us, not *where* it happened. Would it have been any less effective had it occurred in Canada? Stunned at what they perceived as irreverence, they offered to pay the $300 airfare to get Jesus back to Israel from Canada. True to his word, I received a check from my father shortly thereafter. In the memo section he wrote, "To Preserve Calvary!" I quickly made it into confetti, but agreed not to rewrite history and called the publisher to pull the book and make the change – just another Lucille Ball moment to add to my growing list of comedic episodes. I believe there is only one collector's edition available, which I gave to my surgeon for posterity.

While I may not always get the words or the punctuation right, I hope the meaning shines through loud and clear.

Despite our imperfections, we can all 'author' our own story, which is all we have to offer anyway. There are no perfect lives, so how can there be perfect stories? The humor and the lessons are always found in our mistakes and in our willingness to correct them. Far be it for me to be the exception to this truth. So, while I am sure you will find other errors that I missed, it is my hope that my story touches you in some way that reveals the beauty of God's love, which can be found anywhere and which transcends all boundaries, including geographical ones.

I Don't Buy Green Bananas

If you can't be a good example –
then you'll just have to be a horrible warning.
Author Unknown

While recuperating from my first cancer surgery, I decided to compile a book of stories from people who, like me, were given a second chance at life. It was going to be called *The Mulligans* and would begin with my own experience. However, during this time I picked up a book given to me by a friend, *Kitchen Table Wisdom*. Apparently, someone had beaten me to it and done it much better than I could ever have hoped. It changed my life because it encapsulated my feelings so beautifully. Each chapter recalls a different person's encounter with cancer. Some survived, some did not. Nevertheless, the resounding theme was that getting cancer was the best thing that ever happened to them. Only under the threat of death did they truly learn how to live, whether it be for days, weeks, months, or years. Along with the diagnosis came an inexplicable calm and, as crazy as it sounds, joy.

However, after finishing the book I now wouldn't have to write, *The Mulligan* idea still lingered. Then it occurred to me that people who have escaped death aren't so special even though we've certainly been given a gift. By its very nature, life itself is a terminal illness, and we are all granted

5

a mulligan every morning we wake up. Every day's a "do-over," a new opportunity to get it right, to change, to grow, to correct a mistake, to do things differently, to live in the moment. Maybe there was a book there after all.

I first heard the term mulligan from my husband, who is a golfer. Why he is a golfer remains a mystery to me. More often than not he comes home frustrated and discouraged, yet he eagerly continues to go back for more. Avid golfers explain that it's the times when all goes right that keep you coming back. Those times when the planets align and you shoot the perfect game. Not unlike life I suppose. When you get it right, when you are aligned with God's purpose for you, there is no better feeling. It's what keeps us going, frequently frustrated and discouraged, but determined to achieve our own heavenly hole-in-one. Bob may never achieve his fantasy of the perfect swing during his lifetime, and neither will any of us discover spiritual nirvana here on earth. Still, it sure is fun trying.

Before I had the opportunity to explore the mulligan idea further, I discovered that my cancer had returned and was probably establishing permanent residency. I didn't have time to delve into the mulligan concept; hence, the birth of *I Don't Buy Green Bananas.*

A popular phrase amongst the geriatric set, this adage can be applied to anyone who doesn't plan on a long-term future. I've seen it employed in songs, books, insurance ads, sermons, and in medical parodies. What the title lacks in imagination, it more than makes up in clarity. It conveys the clear message to live in the moment. I believe the younger generation prefers the less foreboding "carpe diem" or "seize the day," which, I was dismayed to learn, can be interpreted as "eat, drink and be merry, for tomorrow we die." In fact, Wikipedia directed me to the following verses in the Bible, clearly illustrating the danger of quoting scripture out of context.

> *'Let us eat and drink,' you say,*
> *'for tomorrow we die.'*
> *Isaiah 22:13b*

> *Let us eat and drink,*
> *for tomorrow we die.*
> *1 Corinthians 15:32b*

For someone allotted an extra helping of the fun gene, this might be construed as a hall pass for debauchery. Read in context, however, it is what comes before and after those verses where the real message lies. Isaiah's prophecy concerns God's judgment for lack of repentance. In it, the people lose hope under the threat of attack and rather than repenting and turning to God, they give in to despair and self-indulgence with dire consequences.[1]

In a similar fashion, neither is Paul promoting merrymaking in his letter to the Corinthians. He, too, is issuing a warning as the next verse reveals.

> *Do not be misled.*
> *'Bad company corrupts good character.'*
> *Come back to your senses as you ought,*
> *and stop sinning:*
> *for there are some who are ignorant of God.*
> *1 Corinthians 15:33-34*

Since we are not privy to God's agenda, we need to live each day in such a way that we will be prepared for His coming. Based on the anonymous quote I began with, it is obvious where I see myself in God's plan. *"If you can't be a good example – then you'll just have to be a horrible warning."* I am a walking reminder that you never know when you will suddenly and unexpectedly be faced with your own mortality. It is this fact that Paul and Isaiah were emphasizing. Stop merrymaking and make sure you are right with God because tomorrow may never come. In addition, Isaiah's prophecy stressed the importance of trusting in God always and not our own devices, so that we don't sink into despair when we find ourselves in a situation where we have no ability to save ourselves.

Despite the fact that the doctors are confident my cancer will return, they don't know when. Well, we know Christ is coming back too, but we don't know when either. The way I see it, my job is to live like they're both coming tomorrow.

I realize many people may think it narcissistic to write books about oneself. I don't see it that way. I'm just following some sound advice offered repeatedly throughout my life; namely, "Stick with what you know." I can't claim expertise on many things, but I do know myself. I just use my own life to illustrate brokenness and redemption in its many forms. If there is one thing you can say about humans, it's that we are incredibly slow learners, and we are more alike than we care to admit. We're still struggling with the same issues since Adam and Eve were banished from Eden. The names and faces change, but the sins remain stubbornly rooted in the depths of our souls. You could say I have a PhD in being an FHB (fallible human being.) I finally discovered an area in which I excel. It is also the beauty of recognizing God's grace offered each day as a mulligan: a divine "do-over."

The fact remains: I don't know how many "do-overs" I have left, so I'd like to share with you my journey. One of my daily devotionals said it best, "Sit down and rest in the ride of God, our Father, carrying us home to Him."[2]

Here is trustworthy saying that deserves full acceptance:
Christ Jesus came into the world to save sinners —
of whom I am the worst.
But for that very reason I was shown mercy so that in me,
the worst of sinners,
Christ Jesus might display His unlimited patience
as an example for those who would believe on Him
and receive eternal life.
1 Timothy 1:15-6

Trouble with Tribbles

Praise be to the God and Father of our Lord Jesus Christ,
the Father of compassion and the God of all comfort,
who comforts us in all our troubles,
so that we can comfort those in any trouble
with the comfort we ourselves have received from God.
2 Corinthians 1:3-4

The Christmas season of 2007 marked the start of what I refer to as a road trip with God. If you think about it, our entire life is a road trip with God, but every once in a while he takes you on what might seem like a detour, but is really an excursion. The difference between normal day-to-day cruising and a road trip is that on a normal day I am so busy trying to wrestle the steering wheel away from God, I frequently miss what God is trying to teach me. When you are intent on driving, you can't enjoy the ride, take in the scenery, or fully appreciate your surroundings. On an excursion, God doesn't even let you in the front seat. Like it or not, you are along for the ride; and you'd better buckle up, because excursions are rarely a smooth journey. Not only that, you'd better have a good stock of roadies along as well – and not the kind you stack on ice. The types of roadies you'll need are the ones provided by the Holy Spirit, which come with free refills.

My particular road trip began on an ordinary day crowded with mundane tasks and responsibilities. It's funny, I can't remember what I had for breakfast today, yet I can remember the smallest detail of that day. Honestly, I knew before I walked into the doctor's office that there was something in my belly. Never being the proud owner of rock hard abs, I now found one side of my stomach quite firm while the other side remained the doughy mass I'd come to know and love.

Anyway, I showed the doctor this phenomenon, and the look on her face confirmed that we were discussing something serious. She immediately sent me for a sonogram followed by a CAT scan, which confirmed that I was the proud parent of what I affectionately named a tribble. For those of you who are too young or never were *Star Trek* fans, a tribble is a round, adorable, furry pet.

> The 'trouble' with the tribbles is that they reproduce far too quickly; and threaten to consume all the onboard supplies. The problem is aggravated when it is discovered that the creatures are physically entering essential ship systems, interfering with their functions and consuming any edible contents present. (*Sounds eerily familiar to a malignant tumor.*)
>
> Captain Kirk realizes that if the tribbles are getting into the *Enterprise's* stores, then they are a direct threat to the grain stores aboard the station. However, upon examining the holds, Kirk learns that it is already too late; the tribbles have indeed eaten the grain. It appears the mission has ended in a fiasco. Spock and McCoy, however, soon discover that around half the tribbles in the hold are dead and many of the rest are dying, alerting the Federation that the grain has been

poisoned. Furthermore, the tribbles also give away the identity of a Klingon agent responsible. The saboteur is the only 'human' the tribbles don't like. Upon a medical scan by Dr. McCoy, it is revealed that Darvin is indeed a Klingon in disguise. Thus the tribbles redeem themselves and enable the Federation to score a diplomatic victory against the Klingons.[3]

The official diagnosis was a ten-inch malignant tumor called a retroperitoneal liposarcoma. You may think it a stretch, but even though it's been at least 30 years since I've seen that episode, when I looked at the perfectly round mass on the sonogram, I immediately thought of a tribble. What's more, two weeks later, on our way back from our annual family trip to the Poconos, the newscaster on the radio announced that it was the anniversary of *Star Trek's Trouble with Tribbles* episode. What are the odds of that? I can't say I discovered any Klingons at Sloane, but my tribble also redeemed itself by presenting me with many blessings before its extraction.

In any event, on that fateful day, after leaving the doctor's office, I went directly to where most children go when they are hurt – to a parent. My favorite place to visit and talk with God is in the chapel of my church. It is quiet, peaceful, and you can almost feel His calming presence. I never fail to find comfort and rest there. We always refer to God as our Father, but I've always felt He embodies attributes of both a father and a mother. Being a supreme being, I doubt He has a gender, but we as humans have to fit Him into our own frame of reference. If, in fact, we are all made in His image, He must be a combination of both male and female traits. Either way, it was to this parent that I ran.

I prayed – not for a miraculous cure, but for the courage and strength to face whatever challenges lay ahead. It being the Christmas season, I looked to Mary as an example and let my prayer be, "May it be to me as you have said." and "Jesus, I trust in you." In the chapel there is a large portrait of Jesus with one hand on his heart, and the other appears to be blessing you. His heart is radiating, drawing you into His loving embrace. Underneath is the simple inscription "Jesus, I trust in you." Whenever I find myself in difficult or unfamiliar circumstances (and this was certainly one of those), I use this picture as a visual and pray these simple words, "Jesus, I trust in you." Though the prayer is simple, it embodies the essence of my faith. It's not that I will only trust Him if I am healed or if things go my way; but, more importantly, I can trust that wherever I am and whatever happens, He can and will help me through.

I can do everything through him who gives me strength.
Phillipians 4:13

But the Lord stood at my side and gave me strength.
2 Timothy 4:17a

So do not fear, for I am with you;
do not be dismayed, for I am your God.
I will strengthen you and help you;
I will uphold you with my righteous right hand.
Isaiah 41:10

While sitting in the chapel, I was filled with a peace that transcends human understanding. I knew without a doubt that

I was not going to die from my tribble – at least not now. I
don't know if it will grow back or ultimately prove to be fatal.
The peace I was filled with wasn't because I was guaranteed a
good outcome; it was because I understood that He would take
care of my family and me *regardless* of the outcome. I didn't
need to be afraid. That confidence helped me strengthen and
encourage my family who didn't necessarily share my peaceful
attitude. I took his command "Be not afraid." quite literally,
mentally buckled in, and gladly responded, "Okay, let's go!" I
was never scared, nor do I suffer from a malady that befalls
many cancer patients; namely, the fear that any new ache or
pain is the beginning of a recurrence, despite the fact that
the surgeon informed me that there is a greater than 50%
chance that my tribble will return. There is a reason Christ
repeats this command so often throughout the Bible (366
times to be exact). I believe it was one of the most important
concepts He wanted to teach us because He knew firsthand
how frightening a place this world can be.

For I am the LORD, your God,
who takes hold of your right hand
and says to you,
Do not fear; I will help you.
Isaiah 41:13

So we say with confidence,
"The Lord is my helper; I will not be afraid."
Hebrews 13:6

Do not be afraid, for I am with you.
Genesis 26:24

Take courage! It is I. Don't be afraid.
Matthew 14:27

Don't be afraid; just believe.
Mark 5:36

Do not let your hearts be troubled
and do not be afraid.
John 14:27b

Though I'd never found myself in a situation as serious as this before, there have been plenty of others where I have experienced a lack of control (divorce, infertility, job loss). When I find myself in a situation where I have no power or authority, I enter a God zone. It's a place I retreat to when circumstances are beyond my control or beyond my ability to deal with them. It's a good place to be. It is an out-of-body experience where I find myself doing things I would never believe possible. I know what needs to be done, and I do it without thinking about the battle, the odds, or the outcome. I can rest in the confidence that God can and will get me through despite how difficult circumstances may appear. This doesn't mean it won't be difficult or painful. It simply means He will be carrying me every step of the way providing whatever strength and endurance is needed. Heroic people aren't necessarily born with extraordinary strength or courage. No, God doesn't give you the strength until you need it. This way there is no mistaking its source. One of my daily devotionals the week before surgery read, "Our greatest strength is often shown in our ability to stand still and trust God."

It is God who arms me with strength
and makes my way perfect.
Psalm 18:32

The Lord will fight for you;
you need only to be still.
Exodus 14:14

The funny (and best) thing about my God zone is that it blessedly prevents me from realizing the severity of the situation. I simply give it over to God, and let Him worry about it. Only when the crisis is over and reality sets in do I grasp the gravity of the situation. My tribble is a perfect example. I remember while at Sloane attending an evening of comedy. Sadly, I was one of only three attendees who shuffled down to the Recreation Room with IV poles in tow. The comedians performed anyway for our benefit. When I say they were bad, it is a gross understatement. I would rather have been having another tribble-ectomy than sit through another act. However, I felt so sorry for them, I didn't have the heart to leave. How did I know they would take my entrance comment seriously? "Don't make me laugh too hard because it hurts!" As bad as I felt for them, I recognized in their faces the sympathy and compassion they felt for me. I wondered, "Why are they looking at me like that? I'm not that sick." Then again, I looked around and was reminded that this was a cancer institute, not the Poconos.

One of my favorite gifts prior to surgery was a prayer shawl. It was made by some women at my parents' church who sent it with the following message.

Woven into this prayer shawl are prayers for
courage, hope, strength, trust and faith.
When you wrap yourself in this shawl,
we pray that you will feel the Lord's arms around you
filling you with His comfort and peace.

While wearing it, I couldn't help but feel wrapped in God's love. It was and continues to be a source of great comfort. It arrived with the following prayer attached:

Heavenly Father,
I call on you right now in a special way. It is through
your power that I was created. Every breath I take,
every morning I wake, and every moment of every
hour, I live under your power.
Father, I ask you now to touch me with that same
power. For if you created me from nothing, you can
certainly recreate me. Fill me with the healing power
of your spirit. Cast out anything that should not be in
me. Mend what is broken. Root out any unproductive
cells. Open any blocked arteries or veins and rebuild
any damaged areas. Remove all inflammation and
cleanse any infection.
Let the warmth of Your healing love pass through
my body to make new any unhealthy areas so that my
body will function the way You created it to function.
And Father, restore me to full health in mind and
body so that I may serve You the rest of my life.
I ask this through Christ our Lord.
Amen.

As you can see, the prayer calls for God's healing power in a physical sense. I knew the doctors at Sloane (under God's wisdom and guidance) would take care of my physical well-being. I was more interested in the biopsy I needed on my soul and God's surgical skill in removing years of regrets, resentments, bitterness, anger, pride, selfishness, jealousy, guilt, etc. The removal of these malignancies was more vital to my future than the loss of any organ because their continued growth would choke out the ability to see or fulfill God's purpose for me. My tribble-ectomy satisfied both. Following the surgery, I really did feel as if I'd been *(gasp)* born again.

Despite the much maligned term, I have a newfound appreciation for the concept of being "Born Again." There is no doubt I was being given a second chance at life, and when you've been blessed like this, you can't help but look at things in a whole new light. I've always avoided tackling the dreaded "Born Again" topic because it offends so many people. I don't know how this term became so taboo. Obviously, Jesus doesn't mean that we have to literally be born again. He simply means that when we are spiritually awakened, we perceive and understand life in a whole new way. In fact, by definition, becoming a Christian *is* being born again. As C. S. Lewis states, "When you accept Christ in your life, you let him move in." Only then does the renovation begin.

It's similar to when you get married. When you're single, it's all about you. You don't have to worry about anyone else's opinions, likes, dislikes, etc. You can do anything you want, wherever, whenever, and however you want, without having to answer to anyone. After you get married, your life is changed permanently. Anyone entering into a marriage expecting to maintain their single lifestyle is doomed to failure. You can no longer put yourself first. When and if you have children, it starts all over again, and your life changes forever yet again. For the most part, people entering into a marriage or becoming parents understand they are about to embark on a new journey and eagerly embrace their new lifestyle. The change is welcome. For me, I've always thought marriage and parenthood has made me a better person. My spouse brings out what's best in me. And so it is with Jesus.

When you truly accept Jesus' love and sacrifice on your behalf, you can't help but be changed forever (born again). His love and grace permeate your entire being altering your desires, decisions, and direction. You don't want to be the same person you were. Contrary to what some believe, this doesn't mean that you'll immediately transform into a bible-thumping, tee-totaling zealot going door-to-door trying to convert people. There are plenty of fun, normal (or as close to it as humanly possible) people who have experienced the phenomenon of being born again. It doesn't necessarily mean they abandon all their vices (though some do). It just means we recognize Jesus as our savior and that He comes first and foremost in our lives. It is simply a reordering of love. The acronym JOY (Jesus, Others, Yourself) describes this new order, and when aligned properly, can't help but fill you with happiness, contentment, and the Holy Spirit.

Therefore, if anyone is in Christ,
he is a new creation;
the old has gone, the new has come!
2 Corinthians 5:17

I tell you the truth,
no one can see the kingdom of God unless he is born again.
John 3:3

For you have been born again,
not of perishable seed, but of imperishable,
through the living and enduring word of God.
1 Peter 1:23

We should all suffer from a serious illness once in life just so you can realize how much you're loved and experience the miracle of being given a new lease on life. If I wasn't so uncomfortable, I could have gotten used to all the attention. My kids were doing everything I asked, I didn't have to yell, I didn't have to cook, and I was getting mail, emails, and phone calls from people who were not trying to sell me something. After I discovered I needed to have surgery and the surgeon assured me I would lose at least 15 lbs., I decided I might as well make the most of the three weeks before my hospital stay. So I threw caution to the wind and ate and drank anything I wanted. I felt like Queen Latifah in the movie *Last Holiday*, where an MRI determines her character, Georgia Byrd, has only three weeks to live. Unbeknownst to her, she was given the results of someone else's test. Thinking she only has a short time left, she abandons her safe, predictable lifestyle, takes all her money out of the bank and "goes on her dream vacation to the Grandhotel Pupp in the spa city of Karlovy Vary, Czech Republic."[4] While *Woodloch Pines* in the Poconos is a far cry from the Grand Pupp, at least I didn't miss the annual Family Olympics.

Like most of us, Georgia Byrd is an ordinary woman with an ordinary job living an ordinary life. However, she secretly keeps a scrapbook labeled the *Book of Possibilities* chronicling her hopes and dreams. Personally, I'm just too lazy to go to the effort, but I used to keep a mental scrapbook of the same kind of things. However, the closer I draw to God, the more I rely on Him to compile my *Book of Possibilities* because I could never have imagined His plans for me. The confines of my own humanity prevent me from seeing beyond my own limited imagination or agenda.

No eye has seen, no ear has heard,
no mind has conceived what God has prepared
for those who love Him.
1 Corinthians 2:9

God's plans have surpassed anything I could have anticipated. Keep in mind, they are frequently not easy to understand. On more than one occasion I've been known to cry out in horror, "That's your plan?!" This detour was no exception. "God, I know I asked you to help me lose weight, but surely there has to be an easier way."

For I know the plans I have for you,
declares the LORD,
plans to prosper you and not to harm you,
plans to give you hope and a future.
Jeremiah 29:11

Over the years God has permanently altered my own silly ideas of success and replaced them with the Godly definition of a successful life. Believe it or not, it is a lot easier to achieve success in His eyes than worldly success. And even though worldly success has its perks, it can never compare to the high you experience when you discover and follow God's plans for you. Furthermore, worldly success can be fleeting, but no one can take away the permanence of your relationship with your Father. This doesn't mean that they are mutually exclusive. Many times God uses our worldly successes as part of His plan for us and others. Queen Esther is a perfect example of someone who used her position and influence for God's purpose of saving the Jews from annihilation.

> *Who knows but that you have come to*
> *royal position for such a time as this?*
> *Esther 4:14b*

During my illness and recovery (which I am happy to say is behind me for now), I received a number of cards and notes where people expressed what an inspiration I was to them. It's funny, I've never felt like the type of person that could ever inspire anyone, but I guess the same could be said of so many people you read about in the Bible. Jesus didn't choose the lofty, charismatic leaders to reveal His divinity. He used ordinary, lowly, needy people so that His power would be obvious in their transformation. I may not feel inspirational; but ordinary, lowly, and needy are feelings to which I can relate. Yes, he uses everyone's abilities for His purposes, but what He wants us to know is that we can all inspire regardless of our abilities or lack thereof. Look at the anointing of Jesus in Mark 14:8 and Matthew 26:13. Mary's (Lazarus' sister) simple act of love has been recorded in history as inspiration for generations of Christians. She didn't accomplish great things or enjoy worldly success. However, she was able to succeed in the one thing that Jesus values above all else. Christ asks only that we love Him and live so others see that love.

I tell you the truth,
wherever the gospel is preached throughout the world,
what she has done will also be told, in memory of her.
Mark 14:8

One might question God's timing in my circumstances, but even here His hand was evident. As my cousin astutely pointed out, because it was Christmas God knew I would be surrounded by my family who would help me through this crisis. It is unbelievable that in the span of one month I was diagnosed, underwent surgery, and was already recovering. It is a mystery to me how people without doctors in their family navigate their way though the healthcare quagmire. Again, I was blessed by having two sisters walk me through the system and help me digest all that was being thrown at me.

One of the many lessons I learned from my experience is when you pray for God's help, He often answers by giving you a job. He remained true to form in responding to my request. While I lay in my hospital bed praying for healing, He gave me a job for which I am eternally blessed. I don't relay the story to make myself look saintly, but to illustrate that God can use you even at your worst. It's one of His favorite methods of healing and no more miraculous than making the lame walk or the blind see.

O Lord my God,
I called to you for help and you healed me.
Psalm 30:2

Rest assured, there is always a reason in the situation we find ourselves, though usually not evident to us. Even in the most difficult circumstances, God will give you a purpose.

My assignment came in the form of my new neighbor, John. He was an elderly man suffering from Parkinson's and leukemia. His particular ailment that night was some sort of blockage, which apparently is extremely painful. As I lay in my bed, I heard him being moved into his room late one night and couldn't help but hear him moaning loudly in pain. Considering all the medications I was on, the clarity of purpose I felt at that moment could only come from the Holy Spirit. I knew God wanted me to go comfort this man. John and I spent the night together. The only thing I had to offer was a foot rub and a listening ear. So he talked while I rubbed. He told me about his life and his family while the lonely hours of night crept closer to dawn. When he thought it was a decent enough hour, I used my cell phone to call his sons so he could talk to them. During those hours John had me get the nurses quite a bit. He'd ring the buzzer, and if they didn't come fast enough, he'd have me go rap on the window of the nurse's station. Before she left for the day, the night nurse stopped in to gently chide us for being such a nuisance all night. Most of the time I spent with John was in the dark until sunrise. By early morning, his caregiver, Cecilia, arrived along with a battery of doctors. I knew my presence was no longer needed.

I returned to my room and took a shower and washed my hair for the first time in a week, signifying a major milestone for me. When I went to check on John later in the morning, he looked at me with a surprised expression and said matter of factly, "I didn't realize you were so beautiful." At that moment, standing by his bed in my new Costco pajamas, for one of the few times time in my life, I did feel beautiful, and not because of any makeup tricks they tried to teach me in the hospital. I thought of one of my daily devotionals from earlier in the week. "Nothing is more attractive than being like Jesus." It goes on to say, "Christlike kindness can open the door for a heart-touching testimony. No we're not Jesus, but we *can* try to be *like* him." A servant's attitude is the only beauty application I needed to learn that day.

I was only there for a couple of more days and checked on John often. He told me I saved his life that night. Whatever I did certainly wasn't my doing, but John did live long enough to say goodbye to his children in person. We didn't know each other long, but I know God put us together to get John through a long, lonely, painful night and to demonstrate that He still had work for me to do. It was a turning point in my recovery and the most effective pain reliever I could have hoped for because it didn't cause nausea. John died on my birthday shortly after I left the hospital, which made our night together all the more meaningful. God didn't want him to be alone or afraid as He approached the end of his life.

Though John had told me that he was a doctor, from his obituary, I learned that "he was a brilliant and world-renowned pediatric radiologist who authored over 150 journal articles and gave over 90 presentations throughout the world. A celebrated teacher, he inspired many students to become pediatric radiologists." Even in death, God used him to teach me a valuable lesson on the importance and beauty of having a servant's heart.

Since learning of John's death from his doorman when I arrived for a surprise visit, I have beaten myself up for not talking to him about God during our night together. On the other hand, the more I thought about it, I firmly believe if that's what God wanted me to do, I wouldn't have been able to remain silent. I was sent to love him by comforting him and listening to him – sometimes *that is* God's greatest witness. There is no doubt that the inexplicable love I felt and still feel towards this stranger could only come from God. I don't even know if John was a Christian. If he was, I'm sure he recognized God's presence that night. If he wasn't, maybe he felt God's presence for the first time.

At the end of any road trip with God, I am filled with mixed emotions. On the one hand, I am grateful I survived the trip and am anticipating moving forward. But at the same time, I want to cling to the intimacy I've enjoyed during the journey even as God gently prompts me back into day-to-day life. I know it sounds weird – almost like I don't want to get better. The only analogy I can think of is putting your child on the bus for the first day of kindergarten. You can see it in their eyes that, even while they are excited to embark on this new adventure, they are tempted and often do cling to the safety of their parents' arms. Some have more trouble than others breaking away from the security of home or God. Eventually, however, we all let go and face the world with all its challenges, bringing with us the lessons learned on our excursion. I, too, go reluctantly but not empty-handed. I am filled with His presence to share with others. It is always one of His purposes for the trip.

*Praise be to the God and
Father of our Lord Jesus Christ,
the Father of compassion and the God of all comfort,
who comforts us in all our troubles,
so that we can comfort those in any trouble
with the comfort we ourselves have received from God.*
2 Corinthians 1:3-4

In closing, I will share with you the most important lesson I learned from my 'trib'ulations. One of the haunting doubts that has plagued me over the years, and especially since I've started writing, is whether this faith I write about so freely could withstand a major challenge. It's like reading a parenting book written by someone who doesn't have kids or whose parenting skills you question. After all, I had yet to suffer anything traumatic, but have found my faith shaken at times under some pretty trivial things. Maybe that was the *soul* purpose of my tribble – to teach me that they aren't just words and to remind me that my faith is a gift from God, so how could I question its veracity. My faith not only withstood the challenge but grew proportionately with each new obstacle.

For it is by grace you have been saved, through faith –
and this not from yourselves, <u>it is the gift of God</u> –
not by works, so that no one can boast.
Ephesians 2:8-9

When all is said and done, I wouldn't forego my 'trib'ulations for anything. I consider it a privilege to be broken because only then can you experience the beauty and miracle of being made whole again. My tribble has brought me so many blessings, the best of which is an intimacy with God as I rest in the shelter of his arms.

The eternal God is your refuge,
and underneath are the everlasting arms.
Deuteronomy 33:27

And we know that in all things
God works for the good of those who love him,
who have been called according to his purpose.
Romans 8:28

As an afterthought to writing this essay, I wondered why I always feel so compelled to share more details about my life than most people probably want to know. In response to an email about my new book, one of my cousins inquired about my health issues. She began, "If you want privacy or don't want to be more specific, that's obviously your call." HA! I directed her to the Caringbridge site, to which she responded. "My earlier question about whether you were trying to maintain your privacy shows that I was momentarily stunned after reading your first e-mail. I should have guessed that there'd be a pool and there'd be photos."

As I was contemplating this, I asked God whether this was what He wanted me to do or had I made it all about me instead of Him? I opened my daily devotional and received God's answer, which I gladly share with you.

What on Earth Are You Doing?

You may have heard that phrase when your mom told you to clean your room and found you playing with your toys instead or maybe when your teacher caught you passing notes in class. But if God were to ask you this question, how would you respond? Paul tells us that as followers of Jesus we have been put on this earth to bring glory to God in everything we do. So what should that look like?

God's glory is the manifestation of all that He is in His unsurpassed, stunning perfection. It is His amazing love, His wide mercy, His deep grace. His glory is seen in His truth, justice, wisdom, and power. To glorify Him means that we have the high privilege of showing Him off in a world that is totally unaware of what He is really like. Acts of mercy to the undeserving, grace to the needy, forgiveness to an offender, living wisely according to His will – all give glorious visibility to the character and quality of our God.

There are a lot of misconceptions floating around about God. It's our job to let others see what He is really like. And, when they like what they see, let's be sure to let them know who taught us to live like that. It's not a good idea to steal God's glory!

May our lives be a 'show and tell' for God's glory.

Joe Stowell
Our Daily Bread

No Place Like Home

If home's where my heart is then I'm out of place
Lord, won't you give me strength to make it through somehow
I've never been more homesick than now.
Mercy Me, 2004

Homesickness is an ailment we all suffer from at some point in our lives. It is not necessarily confined to a childhood camp experience, though I am familiar with that strain. When I was six, I attended a camp run by nuns, and the wicked witch in the black habit confiscated the stuffed animal with which I slept. I never forgave her. Perhaps that is the root of my rebellion against Catholicism.

Regardless, over the years there have been other circumstances that triggered new episodes of homesickness: moving to a new state at 13, leaving home at 18 (though I would never have admitted it then), and leaving New York City to move to the suburbs. However, none has hit me harder than the case I struggle with today.

This new affliction surfaced about five months after my cancer diagnosis and surgery to remove a poison bowling ball from my gut, along with a kidney. It was the best and worst thing that has ever happened to me. I won't sugarcoat the experience. It was, without exaggeration, the hardest physical challenge I've had to date. Even so, after the first four days following surgery, my hospital stay was like a mini vacation. I got to meet new people, do crafts, attend a make-up class, and comedy night. In fact, I was disappointed to miss Friday night Bingo on the day I was discharged. Someone came in to make my bed everyday, and I ordered from room service. I didn't have to share the remote or listen to any bickering. This was not such a bad deal.

The best thing about the whole experience is that it afforded me a glimpse of Heaven. I was enveloped in a cocoon of love by friends, family, and God. His peace saturated my entire being. If you've ever found yourself in the eye of a storm, you'll understand what I mean. Though the storm rages around you, in the eye it is eerily peaceful. It's going to sound weird, but I've never been happier. For someone who has battled depression all her life, this was a new experience, and I liked it. If this is how the rest of the world woke up every day, I had a lot of catching up to do.

I've only felt this kind of intimacy with God on one other occasion: when my friend, Mira, was dying of cancer. In hindsight, I think her death prepared me for my own struggle. God chose to reveal himself at that time so that when I faced the demon myself, I needn't be afraid. Not only was I not afraid, I jealously guarded my newfound intimacy with God. I didn't want people to intrude upon my time with Him, so I kept visitors to a minimum. I refused offers to come pray with me because who needs company praying when you are enjoying some one-on-one time with God? I was in His hands for sure, and He knew my every need. Coming from a large family, it was like the few times I had my parents' undivided attention *without* being in trouble. I didn't know how long this was going to last, so I greedily protected our time together.

The problem was that I got stuck in that peaceful place between both worlds. There is a certain freedom you experience when relieved of your duties. With my daily responsibilities removed, being at peace was easy, and the temptation to linger there was irresistible. However, once the crisis was over and I was faced with the demands of daily life, God's presence and peace evaporated despite my valiant efforts to cling to it. I resisted as much as I could, but as soon as it was determined that I would indeed live to see another day, my grace period ended abruptly. I even started getting calls for volunteering. I thought for sure one of the upsides to this episode was a much-needed sabbatical from any kind of volunteer work. At least I now had a legitimate excuse for responding to those requests with an emphatic "No." Nevertheless, after a month of blissful peace, I found myself thrust back into daily life as an unwilling participant, which brings me full circle to my current case of homesickness.

The reason I even attempt to describe the phenomenon of being in community with Christ is so that you will understand how the loss of it made my heart ache. The only way I can describe it is a holy longing to be back in the protective arms of my Father. I realize now that I have suffered from this malady most of my life, but it was never diagnosed. How could I know it was homesickness when I didn't even know what I was homesick for? All I know is that I have always felt a little like Dorothy landing in Oz. My journey along the Yellow Brick Road has been fraught with just as many mishaps as Dorothy and her three friends. I've been imprisoned by own monkeys; namely, my regrets, resentments, bitterness, anger, pride, selfishness, jealousy, guilt, and insecurities. I know I had a brain, but looking back at my litany of bad choices, it's clear I wasn't using it. My spirituality was incapacitated by rust for much of my life, and I've been paralyzed by fear more times than I can remember. Life was one big twister throwing me around at a frantic pace. Satan was the nemesis that hounded me, tempting me to surrender. And, oh how he must have laughed at some of my lame attempts to resist the urge to lie down in the poppies and go to sleep.

I've always been a beat or two out of step with the rest of the world, and I've often felt as if I were operating on a different plane than everyone else – flying under the radar, so to speak. It's always been as if I didn't really belong, regardless of where I landed at any particular moment. In Paul's letter to the Phillipians, he describes his own struggle with homesickness:

> *For to me, to live is Christ and to die is gain.*
> *If I am to go on living in the body,*
> *this will mean fruitful labor for me.*
> *Yet what shall I choose? I do not know!*
> *I am torn between the two:*
> *I desire to depart and be with Christ,*
> *which is better by far;*
> *but it is more necessary for you that I remain in the body.*
> *Phillipians 1:21-24*

Not unlike so many others, there has always been a void in my life that I tried to fill with all the traditional things: food, work, exercise, good deeds, drugs, alcohol. I even dabbled in the New Age Positive Thinking fad and got sprung at

Lifespring. Despite my efforts, nothing served to calm the restlessness or emptiness I felt until I started studying the Bible. It didn't come as an immediate revelation either. It grew and was nurtured by God and some very patient women over the course of seven years before I finally realized this familiar aching that followed me through life was no longer there because I had finally discovered the missing piece to the puzzle of my soul. For once, everything made sense. It was a huge relief to learn I wasn't crazy – misguided or lost would be a better description. In fact, my life has been one long detour off God's chosen path for me. The peace I was searching for wasn't going to be found anywhere but in the arms of God. As Dorothy and her friends discover at the end of *The Wizard of Oz,* "they already had what they had been searching for all along." Glinda's response to their query as to why she didn't tell Dorothy how to get home sooner resonates with truth and wisdom regarding any spiritual journey and discovery. She explains, "Because she wouldn't have believed me. She had to learn it for herself."

God puts a piece of Himself in each of us, and I firmly believe until we tap into that well and draw from His deep reservoir of peace and love, we will always feel restless and unfulfilled regardless of our accomplishments – much like the wizard floating aimlessly in his balloon. A man without a continent is how he describes himself. He just goes where the wind takes him. My trip over the rainbow taught me, like Dorothy, that "The next time I go looking for my heart's desire, I won't look any further than my own backyard; if it's not there, then I never really lost it to begin with."

The other revelation I had was that, along my own journey, I pick up travelling companions, just like Dorothy. Where would her friends be if she had not come skipping along? The Scarecrow would still be stuck on a spike in the middle of a cornfield, the Tin Man would be immobilized by rust deep in the forest, and the lion would still be cowering behind a tree, bullying others to mask his own fears. Just as God plans for us, together Dorothy's entourage managed to find their hearts' desires. And, oh what a time they had. Despite many setbacks and frightening experiences, they enjoyed the journey. In the midst of adversity, they encouraged each other to face their worst fears and carry on. Can you ever forget them holding up the trembling lion as they appeared before the wizard? That is what we are called to do for each other. Perhaps life is just a long journey home, and we are all here to help each other find our way. It is merely the process of finding our own Yellow Brick Road. Which brings up the ubiquitous question, "Do all roads lead to Heaven?" In his novel, *The Shack*, William Young's Jesus responds, "Not at all. Most roads don't lead anywhere. What it does mean is that I will travel any road to find you."[5]

Dorothy's ability to get home was with her all along, and so was mine. My ruby slippers weren't on my feet but in my soul, and they had the power to not only reveal where I belong but get me there as well. As much as he tried, Satan couldn't rob them from me, only I had the ability to deny their existence and their power.

For I am sure that neither death nor life,
nor angels nor rulers,
nor things present nor things to come,
nor powers, nor height nor depth,
nor anything else in all creation,

> *will be able to separate us from the love of*
> *God in Christ Jesus our Lord*
> Romans 8:38-39

Were Dorothy's friends sad to see her leave? Were they tempted to want her to stay? Were they losing something precious to them? Yes, to all of the above. I think the Tin Man said it best when Dorothy was leaving: "Now I know I have a heart…'cause it's breaking." Still, they knew she needed to go home, even though it was painfully difficult to say goodbye. My prayer is that when it is time for me to go home, I will have helped someone find their heart's desire or recognize their own worth, and that I will have oiled a rusty soul or challenged a fearful heart to trust Christ's message of "Be not afraid." When I've accomplished this, perhaps it will be my time to leave as well.

In any case, the antidote for childhood homesickness might be distraction, but right now distraction was exactly the cause of my unease. I didn't need or want distractions. What I missed was the stillness.

> *"Be still and know that I am God."*
> Psalm 46:10

It took me a while to diagnose my homesickness. I couldn't figure out why I was so melancholy having just escaped death. You'd think I'd be ecstatic. When I finally determined why I was feeling this way, I was then faced with determining the proper treatment. I prayed and talked to God about how selfish I felt wanting to abandon those I love and all my responsibilities to be with Him. As is often the case, He answered with a

Godwink. As I drove past church one day, I read my answer in big bold letters: FIND HOME WHERE YOU ARE. Of course! I didn't have to die to go home. If I was having trouble finding God amongst busyness, it was my job to determine ways to recapture our solitary moments together. Not that being busy and being with God are mutually exclusive. I feel closest to God when I am busy creating whether it be designing, beading, writing, or gardening. It is at those times that I can feel His creative energy flowing freely through me. Each of us has his or her own God-given talents that, when exercised, produce a peace, a feeling of being one with God, a feeling of being exactly where you were meant to be, a feeling of being home. The director of my son's summer camp describes it beautifully…

> The Bible says that each of us is made for a specific purpose, and that the Lord's path for us is narrow. There's something you're supposed to be doing, and when you find it, it's incredible. When you're not doing it, it doesn't matter how much money you make, how much "success" you have, etc. – you're simply not going to find deep contentment, peace or joy.
>
> When you're on the right path, you not only get all these things, but it's even cooler. It's like you're not working at all. Sure, you put in the hours of effort and sweat, but you're simply being the person God created you to be, and doing the things you're gifted in and that you enjoy! If you'll just trust Him, He promises to direct your path, provide for your every need, and give you the desires of your heart.
>
> Mike Arnold, President CTO
> *Sportsmen's Journal*, April 2008

You'd think after a life-threatening experience such as mine and my subsequent bout of homesickness, I'd emerge as a different person. I am, but not in the way you'd expect. I was sorry to discover I am still the same flawed individual, picking up all my bad habits again, only with renewed vigor. My disappointment is that my healing didn't extend to the more serious afflictions that threaten my spiritual life whose value has been made all the more clear to me. The scars on my body pale in comparison to the ones covering my soul from repeated abuse.

So where do I go from here? Home, of course, to my spot at the table where God's love and peace are served in abundance. No, I don't need to die to go home. I just need to be still enough to experience His soothing, loving arms wrapping themselves around me and lifting me into His lap. I now realize how blessed I am that I've been given the opportunity to catch a glimpse of the peace that awaits me. I no longer view my homesickness with sadness but with gratitude because at last I've found my true home. I've never been afraid of dying. Quite the opposite, I was afraid of living. Now I need not fear either because just as Christ says in John 8:14 "I know where I came from and where I am going."

Dorothy was so right. "There's no place like home."

We are always confident,
even though we know that as long as we live in these bodies,
we are not at home with the Lord.
Yes, we are fully confident,
and we would rather be away from these earthly bodies,
for then we will be at home with the Lord.
2 Corinthians 5:6,8 NLT

Deep in the Heart of Texas

He has watched over your journey through this vast desert.
These forty years the LORD your God has been with you,
and you have not lacked anything.
Deuteronomy 2:7b

The following journal of last summer's trip to Texas may seem out of place considering the gravity of my first few chapters. Odd as it seems, the trip was an answer to my prayers – a week of comic relief, rejuvenating spa treatments, and yet another glimpse of God, preparing me for my next death-defying round of cancer tag. I'll try to include just the highlights.

Let me begin by saying Texas may not be the desert, but it sure feels just as hot and will probably be the closest I ever get to one. All I can say is forty years is a long time to wander in that kind of heat. No wonder the Israelites complained so much. I barely lasted ten days. They had Moses leading the way. I had Mapquest *and* air conditioning.

Texas was never on my list of places to see before I die; but ever since Vince Young hit the scene, my son has wanted to visit the Lone Star State. This desire was inflamed when a family from Texas moved in a few houses away. Any time Doug suggested Texas as a family vacation, the rest of us would stare, and in unison respond, "No way." This summer

I told my children that from now on they would have to spend at least one week each summer doing something totally different than they've ever done before. So when Doug's friend, Bradley, came up with the idea of a hunting camp in Texas, my son jumped at the idea. I, on the other hand, did not relish the idea of bringing Doug to Texas. What could I say though? This was certainly something different than anything he'd ever done before. One more thing, Doug and Bradley are notorious for getting themselves into some pretty funny predicaments. Luckily, no one has ever gotten hurt, but now that we were adding guns and knives to the equation, I was not so sure this was a good idea. All the same, I enrolled him and committed to visiting Texas for ten days in July. Everyone thought I was crazy, and I tended to agree.

Ripe for an adventure, my son and I set off for Texas eager to embrace a new culture. Who says you have to travel abroad to discover and learn about other ways of life? We may as well have landed on another planet. I felt like I was sending Doug into the wilderness like the Indians did when a boy reached a certain age not far from Doug's. It was a coming-of-age ritual. The idea was that the young brave left a boy and came back a man. Personally, I like the idea of a Bar Mitzvah better. Too bad I'm not Jewish. Hesitant as I was, I dropped him off and was happy to see that the man to whom I was entrusting my son had all his teeth and was not playing banjo music on the radio. At least Doug had a friend with him, and I would never be further than a few hours away in case of an emergency (of which I could think of plenty).

I spent the first night at a Holiday Inn at the Houston airport before leaving for San Antonio in the morning because everyone assured me there was NOTHING to see in Houston. I took their word for it. That night I enjoyed half of a cow and a vat of water, which is the only way they serve beef and drinks down there. I was just introduced to a Texas-sized meal. It was the best steak I had ever eaten. Maybe this week wouldn't be so bad after all.

Not long into the trip to San Antonio, I began seeing signs for a truckstop called Buc-ees. Then I began seeing them every 1/8 of a mile. Just as I finished laughing over one, the next one would pop up. Let me share a sampling:

Texas' Most Famous Restrooms
It's Potty Time!
Restrooms You've Got to Pee to Believe!
Peeing is Believing!
Use our name – You'll get a good seat.

And those are only the ones I can remember. I called my friend from Texas who told me the owner, Beaver, used to be a neighbor with a great sense of humor. Now I understood the mascot he used touting his infamous toilets. I was tempted to stop, but thought I'd have plenty of chances over the next week so passed by. I never did see another so missed an opportunity to visit Beaver's celebrated toilets. The rest of the ride seemed boring with the absence of Beaver's ads. I felt like I had lost a good friend. The Beaver had kept me entertained for at least two hours.

Texans use billboards as advertising more effectively than in the northeast because so many people spend lots of time in their cars. A captive audience is ripe for the subliminal effects of roadside advertising. Amongst the usual ads, though, there are inspirational messages sprinkled in to keep you on your toes. Some of these read:

> Wake Up on the Bright Side
> Make a Difference in Your Community
> Make Miracles Happen
> Reach New Heights
> Rekindle Your wonder
> Share Your Passion
> Real People, Real Problems, Real Solutions…in Jesus.

Those ads certainly kick started my brain as I drove. I guess even God thinks it pays to advertise. Wasn't it on a sign where He gave me the timely message, "Find Home Where You Are?"

Ordinarily, I'd have liked to have my road trip buddy with me, but this was even a stretch for her. Texas in July is a hard sell. Plus, she couldn't get the time off. Nevertheless, I called her periodically while driving; and being the devoted road companion she is, we enjoyed some lengthy chats as I drove and she sat in her car in the garage pretending to be sitting beside me. It was the next best thing.

I visited all the tourist attractions in San Antonio with the Alamo being my first stop. The next day I drove out to Fredericksburg where my cousin resides. I had called the night before only to find that she was out of town, but I decided to take a ride anyway to see the town. I wanted to confirm that she was really married as we have never actually seen her husband, Kenneth. I drove to where her house should have been and found nothing but a herd of goats.

Aha! She is not only not married, she doesn't even live in Texas! Where have all my Christmas cards been going? I got out to stretch, and the goats all came to take a look. I assume they don't get many visitors. Never before had I enjoyed the rapt attention of so many living things. I felt compelled to say or do something, so I broke out in song. "The hills are alive…" Understandably, they watched me in awe with a puzzled look, and I could almost hear them thinking, "What hills?"

Later, I discovered I had transposed some numbers and went back and found her house, but sadly, not her husband. Now I definitely have to come back again. I'll have to be on my best behavior though, because I was issued a formal warning after being stopped by the police for jaywalking. Apparently, it is okay to bear arms in Texas, but you need to *cross at the green, not in between.* The officer stopped me and informed me that I needed to walk to the corner to cross. Pointing to my destination I asked, "Why would I walk way down there when I want to go over here?" He explained the dangers of crossing in the middle of the street, and I waited patiently for him to finish. I looked at him and said, "Listen, it is 110 degrees. I am not walking two steps further than necessary." I didn't even bother to mention that I could see for miles in either direction, and there wasn't a soul in sight. "You're not from around here, are you?" he asked. How did he ever guess? Without further discussion, I took his advice and got out of town quickly thereafter.

One of my goals on the trip was to ride a mechanical bull, which was harder to find than you'd think. On my last day of exploring San Antonio, I found one in Market Square and went for ride. I attracted quite a crowd, which began hooting and hollering to make it go faster so they could watch this idiotic Yankee humbled. Having conquered the bull, I felt I had done all I needed in San Antonio. I left early the next morning, never imagining what awaited me at the Lake Austin Spa. I eagerly anticipated my deep tissue massage addressing the soreness from my bull ride not realizing just how deep it would truly go. I was about to discover the true meaning of Deep in the Heart of Texas.

I was given a tour of the spa on arrival, including the gym where an instructor told me that classes marked with a diamond are if you really want to sweat – as if I hadn't already perspired three times my body weight over the past few days. I sat down for lunch, looked over the menu and was astonished at the variety of selections and surprised that they would be serving what I would have considered unhealthy or fattening dishes. They listed the calories and fat content, which should have tipped me off that something was amiss. I ordered and enthusiastically awaited a meal in the Texas style to which I had now become accustomed: a vat-sized soda and enough food to feed a small country. A short time later a Texas-sized plate was placed in front of me, but where was the food? I reached for my glasses and low and behold, lost in the center of this enormous dish was a lone bite of my anticipated meal. No wonder they can serve all these delicious items. Nothing is fattening if eaten in mouse-like portions. Clearly, I was going to have to double order or befriend someone in the kitchen if I wanted to survive here. Needless to say, it didn't take long to finish my meal, and I use that term loosely. On to cooking class where I will learn to prepare mouse-sized meals – hardly seems worth the effort. The class is two hours. It took me two minutes to eat: one minute for each bite. At least there is an endless supply of sliced cucumbers to eat without having to sneak them from the bowl outside the steam room.

3:00   God provides. He must have heard my prayers while I was on the treadmill close to fainting from lack of food because, as I passed the living room. I spied two bowls of orzo salad. I learned they supply appetizers everyday between 3:00 and 5:00. So this was the secret. Granted, the bowls provided were the size of sake cups, but no one would notice if I grabbed one of those water cups (which were the standard Texas vat size) and stocked up on "appetizers."

As I was sneaking past the front desk with my stash of orzo, I noticed a sign announcing the Friendship Table. If you want company, you sit at the Friendship Table and hope that someone joins you. Being that this was Day 4 of my solo journey, I thought I'd give it a try at dinner. I wanted to meet some real Texans. However, I arrived in the dining room to find tables full of girlfriends and an empty Friendship Table. It was reminiscent of walking into the lunch room the first day of my new school at age 13. Those awful memories erupted from some reserve I didn't even realize existed. Do I dare sit, announcing to everyone that I was in need of a friend? What happens if no one sits down at this large table? I would feel like a complete loser. I didn't dare take the chance. I'll try again tomorrow. While eating my solitary supper, I couldn't help but eavesdrop on the group of ladies next to me. They weren't discussing anything fascinating until the server arrived to take their dessert order. Every one of them ordered two deserts and one ordered three! These are my kind of women. I was determined to invite myself to their table tomorrow.

I'd done much thinking and soul searching on this trip, still trying to finally digest the events of this past winter and get over my preoccupation with my own death. It was my own sort of spiritual pilgrimage. It was time to stop planning my own funeral and move forward. The best way to do this was to finalize the plans, put them in an envelope and forget about them. The long car rides afforded me ample time to listen to a variety of CDs: one hilarious, some contemplative, and a series of Christian music ones a friend made for me. I don't know if she was trying to tell me something, but she had *Time to Say Goodbye* at least three times along with the tear-jerking *To Where You Are* by Josh Groban. She originally made these CDs for a friend in the hospital, and I was surprised at some of her choices. I was sobbing driving along imagining my husband and children at my funeral. Even so, they did prompt me to finalize the music I wanted for my own service.

Anyway, that first night at the spa when I returned from dinner I found a little card with the following phrases artfully written on it.

> *I release all fears and doubts.*
> *I accept myself and create peace on my mind and heart.*
> *I now choose to free myself from all destructive fears and doubts.*
> *I am loved and I am safe.*

My skin erupted into goose bumps. God is such a show-off sometimes. Of course, He knew I needed that particular card on that particular night to be reminded of His constant presence in my life.

Breakfast the next morning was awesome. Sure, the muffins were the size of a thimble, but if you ate ten of them, you achieved the same effect as a normal-sized one – 20 if you wanted a Texas-sized one. Best of all, I met a friend, Deanne, who asked to join me, even though I wasn't at the Friendship Table. After a few minutes of introductions, she proceeded to tell me that her father hung himself the previous week, and she was now an orphan as he was her last living relative. No wonder she needed a friend. God can use you wherever you are, and this was a call to arms if ever I heard one.

After a morning of relaxation and yoga classes, I decided to try something a little more strenuous and signed up for a group spin class. I arrived at the designated time to learn that it was a group of one, so I got a private class. You might think that was a good thing, but in a group of one there is nowhere to hide. That skinny young thing tried to kill me. "Oh no you don't," I thought, "not before I get to eat lunch." After grabbing my chest gasping for air, she agreed to abbreviate the class from 50 minutes to 30. It took hours for my blood pressure to return to normal. In my nautical noodle class three hours later, women were still asking me why my face was so red.

Noodling was definitely more my speed. Who knew you could do so many things with a noodle? I'd certainly never noodle surfed before. Deanne and I met Phyllis while splashing around and learned she was enjoying a gift from her husband. Two of her four daughters were visiting that day as well. She had two natural daughters and two daughters she adopted and raised as her own when her neighbor died. It takes a special kind of person to do something like that.

She didn't see it that way and thought of her two adopted daughters as blessings.

I went from noodling to a sea salt scrub. Now the rest of my body was as red as my face. On to dinner. I did a little reconnaissance of the dining room through the window to scope out possible seating companions. Both Deanne and Phyllis were seated at full tables, but The Friendship Table had one lone soul at it. I made a beeline toward my new friend, Barbara from Georgia, who had an uncanny resemblance to Betty Davis, which earned her the nickname Betty Barbara. She was also on a chaperone trip. She accompanied her granddaughter with Asperger's to camp and was traveling around waiting to pick her up. She explained that it had taken two hours for the staff at the camp to coax the girl out of the car. What a devoted grandmother, I thought. I need to add one thing here. People in the south run at half speed, so it took a long time for her to eat and get the full story out. I kept hearing my Texas neighbor's voice in my head, "Be nice. People are a lot slower down there." Visiting the cold cut counter at Shaw's had unknowingly been good training ground for my trip to Texas.

Just before we finished, Deanne stopped by the table to say hello. She started telling us how she had decided to use her time here to say goodbye to her Dad and put all her family issues to rest. Before I had a chance to think, the Holy Spirit (always on high alert) prompted me to blurt out, "Why don't we have a candlelight service for him tomorrow night by the lake?" Shocked, she asked, "You'd do that for me?" and tearfully added, "Now I know why I met you yesterday." I was covered with goose bumps as God's answer to what He was preparing me for took shape. I suggested she write down all her family issues on pieces of paper, and one by one we would rip them up and throw them in the lake. Betty Barbara came up with an even better idea. She suggested writing them on rocks to throw them in the lake – brilliant. With that settled, we all said goodnight. I stopped to sit by the lake on the way to my room and remembered the scene in Forest Gump when he accompanies Jenny back to her childhood home, the scene of years of abuse by her father. After she throws her rocks and crumples into an exhausted heap of tears, Forest simply sits down next to her, wraps his arm around her, and in his naive way says, "Sometimes there just aren't enough rocks."

When I returned to my room, I panicked and thought, "What the hell am I thinking? What could I possibly say to this woman to ease her pain?" I prayed my usual "Jesus, I trust in you." I also asked for wisdom and words to comfort Deanne. When I awoke on Wednesday, I kept having the nagging feeling to pull out my daily devotionals from earlier in the week, which I did, and there in black and white was the answer to my prayers. It was a devotional from June 30th, *We Need Each Other to Wait and Weep With*. I will share some of the highlights.

> *Finally, all of you, live in harmony with one another;*
> *be sympathetic, love as brothers, be compassionate and humble.*
> *1 Peter 3:8*

As a pastor, I see situations daily that nobody should ever have to go through alone. Nobody should ever have to wait in the hospital while a loved one is in life-or-death surgery. _Nobody should ever have to stand at the edge of an open grave alone._

Life's tough times and tragedies are inevitable – each of us will face them. But we don't need to go through them alone. We need God's safety net to help hold us up through these difficult times. What is God's safety net? It is a group of other believers – a handful of people who are really committed to you. We call this kind of group a community. Here's God's plan for community: "If one part suffers, every part suffers with it" (1 Corinthians 12:26). Community is God's answer to despair. Romans 12:15 expresses a similar idea: "Rejoice with those who rejoice; mourn with those who mourn."

The first part of that verse is easy. When something good happens to someone, it's often easy to join in on the party. But when someone is having a tough time, it can seem more difficult. But, really, it's simple. *When you're going through a crisis, you don't want advice; you just want somebody to be there – to sit with you, hold your hand, put an arm around your shoulder, or cry with you.*

As Paul tells us, "Therefore encourage one another and build each other up" (1 Thessalonians 5:11 NIV). Encouraging someone else doesn't always mean giving a pep talk or words of wisdom. *Sometimes the best kind of encouragement is just sitting in silence – waiting and weeping with a friend.*

The hard times in life are inevitable, and only a fool would go into them unprepared.

Rick Warren
Purpose Driven Life Daily Devotional
June 30, 2008

When you experience answered prayer in this way, it is more invigorating than a case of Red Bull. It is a reminder from God saying, "Of course I'm here. Haven't I told you a million times I will never leave you, and I am trustworthy. If I give you a job, I will also give you the ability."

I was happy and relieved to now have God's own words for our little service plus the knowledge that God had responded to my daily conversations this week and my repeated requests to "Show me what you want me to do. Here I am." Suddenly, it all became clear to me. I wasn't even supposed to be here. I originally had planned to stay in Austin. My husband had surprised me at the last moment. I could see God's hand in bringing Deanne and me together. Once again, I witnessed that God can give you a purpose in the most unexpected ways and places. You just have to be open to it. Not only that, I remembered an email from my Mom the day before I met Deanne. She was discussing that day's daily devotional, *God Smiles When We Trust Him,* which I hadn't read yet. My response to her proved to be prophetic. I wrote, "I feel I'm being prepared for something but don't know what it is yet – therein lies the adventure!"

When you learn to recognize God, He's hard to miss. In fact, you don't even have to look. Just let Him find you. In the book, *I'm Here if You Need Me,* a forest ranger describes what children do when they realize they are lost in the woods. Instinctively, they find a safe, comfortable spot usually under a bush or similar kind of camouflage, curl up, go to sleep, and wait for their parents to find them. In their innocence they possess the confidence that if they just remain still, they will be found. Wouldn't it be great if we could apply the same logic to God? Why don't more of us take His command to "Be still and know that I am God" to heart. If we could just learn to rest in the confidence that He will find us, life would be so much less stressful. He knows exactly where we are and what we need. I needed a purpose and Deanne needed a friend.

Deanne, Betty Barbara, Phyllis and I met for dinner. To celebrate my last night, I boldly ordered one of each when it came time for dessert. Afterwards, we moved to the dock where I had arranged candles around the edge and gotten a boom box for the music. I took out the sharpies and the rocks Deanne and I had lifted from the various fountains on the property. While we talked, Deanne wrote down the issues she wanted to bury. Betty Barbara and I quietly wrote down our own demons. I chose the more weighty rocks Barbara had mined from a local construction site. Big issues – big stones.

Phyllis asked Deanne to tell us of her favorite memory of her Dad. We listened as Deanne shared stories of her life. We listened to some songs, and I reminded them of the scene from Forest Gump. As sappy as it might seem, I put on the closer, *Time To Say Goodbye*, while we threw our stones into the lake. Deanne began timidly, but we encouraged her to really fling them as hard as she could. It's a great feeling to drown your regrets, resentments, anger, bitterness, fears, etc. I firmly believe we are all in different stages of healing throughout our life. Everyone has their own rocks - some are pebbles, some are boulders. To remember the moment, we all kept one stone Deanne had inscribed with the letter "L." When the stones were gone, we took the roses Barbara had purchased and sprinkled the petals in the lake. It was a gorgeous night with a full, bright moon shining on the water. It was a beautiful scene watching all those delicate rose petals floating across the lake in the moonlight. We hugged as if we had known each other all our lives. There is no doubt in my mind that this was a God moment, a magical wink from God's eye. We all had been brought together for this purpose: to hold someone up in a moment of despair. And in helping her, we ourselves were fed. The true beauty of it was that we all recognized we'd been blessed. Our connectedness with God and each other was obvious. After we said goodnight, I remained on the dock for quite awhile enjoying the night and thanking God for orchestrating it. I also thought that had anyone taken up my invitation to visit Texas in July, I would have missed this opportunity.

Reluctantly, I left the spa the next day. I thought back to the day I arrived. I didn't need to worry about going hungry after all. Here I was three days later feeling quite full, having been fed generously in body and soul.

Austin was a little anticlimactic. In its defense, I must say, God is a hard act to follow. The next morning, I witnessed culinary nirvana at Whole Foods and loaded an assorted array of goodies in the car and hit the road again. There was no need to worry about dozing at the wheel because I had to keep the a/c on max in an attempt to keep the luscious desserts I purchased from melting. All I had to worry about was the windows fogging up. My car closely resembled a rolling version of the old fridge in the shed behind our beach cottage, sweating profusely and forming ice in places. I arrived in Waco blue from the cold.

My husband's nephew and his wife had prepared a warm, Texas welcome for me, complete with a framed Texas flag. I donned the enormous orange cowboy hat I picked up in Austin and rang the bell. Chelsa and JD are the proud parents of five-week old twin girls. As I held them and breathed in their delicious baby scent, I was in awe of the magic and miracle of life. How can anyone hold a newborn and doubt the existence of God?

I've always enjoyed spending time with JD and Chelsa, and this was no exception. Despite her exhaustion from caring for her girls, Chelsa took me on a tour of Waco, which didn't look anything like the Branch Davidian compound I imagined. In fact, it was lovely. It boasted a beautiful lake, an impressive golf course, Baylor University, the Texas Sports Museum, and the Dr. Pepper museum. Chelsa lent me a book titled *Abraham*. Within the first two pages I found the author's answer to suffering, a topic all of us struggle with as we try to determine its meaning and role in our lives. The author says,

> ...wisdom and pain are the twin pillars of life. God pours these qualities into two symmetrical cones, then adjoins them at their tips, so that the abyss of pain meets the body of knowledge. The point where the two cones touch is the center of the cosmos. That point is the Rock, and it's where King David ached to build a Palace of Peace.[6]

It made sense to me and also explained why, in another book I listened to that week, *The Will To Survive*, the resounding theme with many cancer patients is that whether they survived or not, the cancer had taught them how to live. They had gained new wisdom and perspective that they otherwise would have missed. Through their suffering they had reached a new level of living and loving. It also explained the peace that only that place can offer, a peace that I discovered and savored over the winter and remains with me still.

After a lunch of vittles that survived the trip from Austin and heavy with my own food baby, I headed to Crockett. As I got in the car, I received a message from my son that he had gotten a ram the previous night. Not just any ram though. As he described it, his was one of the biggest and the smartest and meanest of them all. I wondered how he knew how smart the ram was. Do they test them before killing them? I guess I'll find out soon enough while I'm eating that smart, mean ram on Sunday!

Crockett, Texas is more like my preconceived idea of the Lone Star state. In fact, it was downright scary. Whoever christened it "Paradise in the Pines" had a vivid imagination. After driving for two plus hours with nothing but cattle for company, I was looking forward to a good steak dinner. At check-in I asked for the location of the local steakhouse. The girl looked at me as if I'd just asked for the closest sushi bar.

> "We only have two places (she didn't even call them restaurants) where you can sit down and eat. A Chinese one on the square and Mexican."
> "Okay, how do I get downtown?"
> "We don't have a downtown."
> *(Be nice I reminded myself.)*
> "Okay, how do I get to the square?"

She gave me directions, and I set off. She wasn't kidding when she said they didn't have a downtown, and now I knew why she called it a square. It wasn't a "square" like we in the northeast would imagine – a place where people went to meet and greet, perhaps with a little gazebo. It was a literal square

– one block north, one block west, one block south and back again of mostly deserted storefronts and the Chinese restaurant she mentioned, which actually didn't look bad. Nevertheless, I'd be damned if I was going to eat Chinese in Texas. Clearly, the "Where's the Beef?" ad must have been born in Crockett. I drove around looking for inspiration. I turned into the Sonic, but it was full of motorcycles, pickups, and a cast of characters that made my old boyfriend, the Hell's Angel, and his comrades look like boy scouts. There were the standard fast-food chains. The Mexican place didn't look safe to enter alone or otherwise, so I settled for the Wal-Mart Supercenter and dinner in my room. I entered Wal-Mart and was bombarded with an enormous display of chemically infused snack food of the 50's: Twinkies, Devil Dogs, Pork Rinds, Snowballs, Whoopie Pies, etc. There wasn't a natural ingredient in the bunch. Let me just say, I was the only one in line buying celery sticks and chicken that wasn't fried or lathered in BBQ sauce. I went back to my room, pulled the table in front of the door and settled in for the night.

Breakfast was interesting. I filled a bowl with something that loosely resembled oatmeal but turned out to be some kind of gravy. No wonder they had it next to the biscuits. After one bite, I thought it would be safer to stick with Cheerios. At least I knew what food group it belonged to. I didn't dare ask for skim milk. It was obvious no one here drank it.

As I looked around, I realized the Holiday Inn didn't cater to the Sonic crowd, and I hadn't needed to barricade my door despite the fact that people kept knocking on it during the evening. These were all families on vacation. Where could they possibly live, if they considered Crockett a destination? It was one of the grannies who took pity on me and kindly let me know I was eating gravy, not oatmeal. As I watched these families happily eating and getting ready for the pool, I chastised myself for profiling and wondered when and how I had become such a snob. Considering some of our destinations as a child, this place looked like the Ritz. My favorite was the Buena Vista Motel because it had a water slide. Then there was the infamous Rosehaven that closely resembled the Bates Hotel. I reminded myself that the middle of nowhere is just that, whether it's in Texas or New Jersey. Oh well, off to the exercise room to dust off the equipment.

When I went back to my room to take a shower, I noticed a familiar sign stating that, due to the popularity of certain amenities, they were offering them for purchase. Ordinarily, they'd be referring to those big fluffy robes in fancy hotels. Here they listed (with prices) the towels, iron, ironing board, hair dryer, coffee machine. I always thought these notices were just a polite way of informing you that if it's missing, you're paying. Who would lift an ironing board, and how would you sneak it out if you were so inclined? You couldn't pass it off as a travel companion because they would be suspicious of anyone that thin here. Next, when I went to look for the shampoo, I found two bottles marked WASH and TAN. Apparently "One Dip Will Do Ya" was also coined in Crockett. This was a full-service washing detergent, which could cleanse and condition both you hair and skin. Saves time, though I haven't met anyone here in a rush.

With the exception of one brief stop to photograph some armadillo road kill, I was at Doug's camp without incident, though I discovered new meaning to "just down the road." I fell in love with the people instantly. All the horrific scenes I had imagined during the week were for naught. They did have a cabin WITH air conditioning and a shower and toilet.

The first words Doug uttered were, "I want to take you to the freezer to show you my ram's head." "Yeeha!" I thought, without realizing there was more. "You can see his balls too!" he exclaimed, using his hands to illustrate just how large they were. Not sure this was really necessary, I wondered if this could be how they had determined his IQ? It would be such a male thing to do. Doug told me they cut off the testicles to eat them, and that they were all lined up in the freezer. Waste not, want not. Two minutes later a man came over with bite-size pieces of ram and offered me an hors d'oeuvre. "What part of the ram is this?" I asked sheepishly (no pun intended). He looked me in the eye and said with a Texas twang, "Parts is parts, maam. Parts is parts." When in Rome, I thought, and dove in. Balls or not, they weren't bad.

We went to the gut shack to visit the freezer. The smell was overwhelming; however, I was the only one gagging while trying to cover my mouth. Then the boys came out dragging their trophies dripping blood, and I thought I was going to lose the mysterious ram parts I just ingested. I poked my head in the trailer-size freezer and saw all the heads lined up, but the balls were nowhere to be found. My stomach lurched.

We chatted with Mr. Chad and Mr. Larry who had been in charge of the boys all week. Again, I was impressed with their devotion and with the insights they gave me about Doug. Mr. Chad highlighted some of the things the boys learned over the week, and not one of them had to do with hunting.

Accountability
Responsibility
Self-Discipline
Listening
Stillness

He considered stillness one of the most important lessons he wanted to leave with the boys. He mentioned how he emphasized that it is important for kids as well as adults to realize that you don't always have to be doing something whether it is work, radio, TV, computer, sports, or any medley of available distractions. It is just as important to have quiet time to think and just talk to each other. In order to truly listen, you have to be still. He went on to say that not listening is really just a form of laziness and that it is easy to become spiritually, physically, and mentally lazy. Mr. Chad was a no-nonsense kind of guy whom I admired for his passion about his faith and his willingness to share it with these youngsters. Yes, he taught them how to hunt, but the more important life lessons they learned while under his tutelage would serve them well in life.

The most impressive sight Doug showed me was the cross he and the boys made and erected at the camp. This thing was huge. As they say, everything is bigger in Texas. I guess this includes God. Judging from the events of my week, I had to agree. It took eleven boys and five men an entire day of work to build it, carry it up the hill, and raise it. They now had a new appreciation for Christ's difficult journey to Calvary. If nothing else, that experience alone would be worth the price of the camp.

Doug got what he came for, plus some. He killed a ram and not just any ram – the biggest, meanest and smartest one there. How he determined that remains a mystery to me, but I'm just going with it. He also learned how to gut it, skin it, prepare it, and eat it. This is a kid who wouldn't even make himself a sandwich.

On the ride to the airport, Doug chatted for a while before he passed out cold. He told me how expensive a well-bred, real nice deer cost. What the heck is a well-bred, real nice deer? Does he have good manners or did he attend sensitivity training? Who knows, but Doug informed me that it costs $5,000 just for his semen. Clearly, good manners go a long way out here in the wilderness. The deer himself costs $70,000. I wondered how humans would be priced. Thankfully, God values us all equally, otherwise I fear I'd end up in the Marshall's of God's economy.

After Doug collapsed from sheer exhaustion, I reviewed what I had learned during my Texas odyssey.

1. You don't need to travel abroad to experience a different culture.
2. Everyone has a story waiting to be told.
3. They aren't kidding when they say "Everything is bigger in Texas."
4. FINDING HOME WHERE YOU ARE IS NOT SO HARD AFTER ALL.

Terror Alert Update

You will not fear the terror of night,
Nor the arrow that flies by day,
Nor the pestilence that stalks in the darkness,
Nor the plague that destroys at midday.
Psalm 91:5-6

So much for comic relief. As I suspected, my Texas trip was preparing me for something, and it wasn't just our night on the dock. Not long after my return, I discovered an unfamiliar lump on my side. Alert status was immediately raised from yellow to a cautionary orange. Then, as I watched it go from the size of a pea to a grape, the level rose again to a screaming red. I was scheduled for a six-month CAT scan shortly, so I decided to wait the couple of weeks to confirm what I already knew. My body was once again under attack.

Since the cancer resurfaced so quickly, the surgeon did not want to operate. I will spare you the tedious, drawn out months that followed, involving endless waiting and consultations with a variety of doctors trying to determine the proper course of treatment. The chapters that follow were written during that uncertain time when I was being offered little hope from the medical community. This is one of the many verses I clung to during that period.

Even though I walk through the valley of the shadow of death,
I will fear no evil, for you are with me;
your rod and your staff, they comfort me.
Psalm 23:4

Say a Little Prayer for Me

The moment I wake up
before I put on my makeup
I say a little prayer for you
                    Burt Bacharach, 1967

No one would argue that prayer is an integral part of our relationship with Christ. Having been raised Catholic, I memorized all the obligatory prayers and recited countless Hail Marys and Our Fathers as penance received at confession. Disobeying your parents? Fighting with your siblings? That will be two Our Fathers, ten Hail Marys, a Glory Be and you're good to go. As a child, the bedtime prayer I was taught to recite was frightful: "If I should die before I wake, I pray the Lord my soul to take." What were they thinking??? No wonder I had nightmares.

This type of prayer has never worked for me because no matter how hard I tried, my mind would start wandering after the first few lines. I perfected the planning of an entire week's worth of menus and grocery lists while praying the rosary. Conversational prayer is my most frequent method of communicating with God, but even that I find limiting. Often, stillness is my most effective means of prayer. The Dixie Chicks' song, *Easy Silence*, comes close to describing my time with God.

And I come to find a refuge in
the easy silence that you make for me
It's okay when there's nothing more to say to me
And the peaceful quiet you create for me
And the way you keep the world at bay for me
the way you keep the world at bay.

Quiet transcends language and creates an opening for a different kind of communication – one where words are not needed. It is in this easy silence where God has the ability to make anyone feel like an only child.

In his infinite wisdom God provides for those of us who struggle with prayer (and who doesn't at some point). In Romans 8:26-27 Paul states:

In the same way, the Spirit helps us in our weakness.
We do not know what we ought to pray for,
but the Spirit himself intercedes for us
with groans that words cannot express.
And he who searches our hearts knows the mind of the Spirit,
because the Spirit intercedes for the saints
in accordance with God's will.

There are days when I stumble over my words, fearful that they might actually be answered just to teach me lesson. You see, my requests vacillate minute to minute, which is why I don't put much stock in them. Historically, I have *never* known what was best for me at any given moment, and God has shown His divine mercy by *not* answering many of my pleas in the manner that I requested. I've been known to pray for something one day (or one minute) then go back the next saying, "Remember what I said? Never mind." There is a life-long string of evidence indicating that *I have no idea what I am doing most of the time.* I can almost guarantee that if I am begging for something, it's probably not what God has in mind. Consequently, I have learned to relinquish my own desires and pray, "Thy will be done. Please help me recognize it, accept it, stop worrying about it, and get out of your way. Amen."

I've never spent much time thinking about the purpose of prayer until recently. After being diagnosed with a serious illness, I've been blessed with many people praying on my behalf. At the same time, I've gotten into interesting discussions regarding miracles and prayer. A number of people offered to come pray with me and over me, which has always made me feel uncomfortable. I explained this to them, and their responses baffled me. I felt as if I were being reprimanded. My thoughts are that if God chooses to heal me, He will do it whether people pray *over* me or not. In fact, He may choose to do it through someone in the medical profession, or someone who is not a Christian, or maybe even through His own gentle touch.

These exchanges prompted me to reevaluate the purpose of prayer. Unquestionably, Jesus wants us in prayer constantly because he wants us in constant community with Him. He wants us to offer our joys, sorrows, fears, and anxieties to Him. Not necessarily so that He can eliminate them, but so He can share them. He is always patiently waiting to help us carry the load and remind us that He is with us by filling us with His peace.

Then Jesus told his disciples a parable
to show them that they should always pray and not give up.
Luke 18:1

And pray in the Spirit on all occasions
with all kinds of prayers and requests.
With this in mind, be alert
and always keep on praying for all the saints.
Ephesians 6:18

Do not be anxious about anything,
but in everything, by prayer and petition,
with thanksgiving, present your requests to God.
And the peace of God, which transcends all understanding,
will guard your hearts and your minds in Christ Jesus.
Philippians 4:6,7

How we pray, however, is as personal as our relationship with Christ and can't be dictated by any person, group, or ideology. Personally, my life is one long conversation with God – sometimes lively, sometimes soft, but most often a comfortable, easy silence.

I have to think that one of the reasons God instructs us to pray and present our needs to Him is that if we weren't always running to Him, hounding Him with our requests, my guess is that we wouldn't run so much. Not only that, we'd probably run out of things to say pretty quickly. God wants us to come to Him much as our own children run to us with skinned knees or maybe a failed test. The best we can do is offer a hug and a band-aid when appropriate, but it comforts them all the same. God doesn't necessarily fix our hurts either, but He does provide His own band-aid of comfort and assurance. Most children are also eager to share their joys as well, and God wants to hear about those too, and everything in between.

I would never suppose to critique anyone's relationship with God. If formal prayers or group prayers draw you closer to Him, I think it's wonderful that you've found that conduit. There is never a wrong way to pray. Our responsibility as children of God is to find the avenues that best help us to develop and nurture our relationship with Him. There are as many different ways to do that as there are people. Why else would there be so many different churches worshiping the same God? I have six siblings who all have a different relationship with our parents because we are all unique. It is no different with God. In turn, He speaks to each of us in a way that only He knows we will understand. There is never just one way because one method might work better in some circumstances than others. Our relationship with God isn't static, nor should our prayers be. In the same way, prayers can't be one dimensional because we're not, and neither is God.

When people began bombarding me with requests to come pray with and over me, I politely declined, responding with sincerity, "It would be an honor to have you pray on my behalf." Much to my surprise, I found myself being chastised. "You don't need to go through this alone," I was reminded. What would make them think that just because I wasn't with them, I was alone? Didn't they understand Christ's message that He would never leave me?

Never will I leave you;
Never will I forsake you.
                    Hebrews 13:5

And surely I am with you always,
to the very end of the age.
                    Matthew 28:20

I've never felt alone. Quite the opposite, I am always trying to carve out solitude. Ask my friends and family. Now I found myself under interrogation as if I denied the power of prayer or the possibility of a miracle, which couldn't be further from the truth. I firmly believe that God will accomplish His will, in His own time, in His own way, whether he has thousands banging on His door or just me whispering quietly in His ear. He doesn't choose to heal everyone, and it's not because He can't or because they didn't pray hard enough. It says specifically in 1 John 5:14 that only *if it is according to his will,* will it be granted.

This is the confidence we have in approaching God:
that if we ask anything <u>according to his will</u>, he hears us.

When I pray, I don't ask for a particular outcome, or for miracles; I pray for wisdom, guidance to recognize God's will, and the peace, courage, and strength to accept it and share what He's given me with others. He never disappoints me, because He always answers by providing exactly what I need at any given moment. Through doctors I learned about this type of cancer and understood all too well that the chance of a cure was remote but not impossible, because

I also know, "nothing is impossible with God." (Luke 1:37) Given the facts, rather than begging for a cure, I needed to be open to the possibility that perhaps the purpose of my life was never to help others learn how to live (and good thing, as I've never been such a good example), but to help them learn how to die. Of course, I intend to pursue any medical treatments available (within reason), but I leave the results or the miracles to God. I also don't approach treatment with desperation to hang on to something God may have chosen to take away. He gave me life, and He alone reserves the right to decide when it ends. I will accept His decision either way with peace and faith that He knows what's best. I've always thought it bordered on arrogance to try and convince God that we know better than He by requesting a certain result. If a cure is part of His plan, He will provide it. I think it pleases Him more to know that I trust and accept His will in all circumstances.

I don't know what my future holds any more than anyone else does in this life. I could get hit by a car tomorrow or die from any number of other things before this cancer has an opportunity to claim my life. Or I could be cured. I pray only that I use whatever time I have left to enjoy every moment of every day and be an example of God's peace and love to my family and anyone else I come in contact with.

A remnant of my Catholic roots, *Here I Am Lord*, has always been one of my favorite hymns. You can't say "Here I Am," then qualify the way in which He uses you. If you truly mean it, you accept whatever you are dealt with grace, humility, and joy and then use it to glorify God, which is exactly what I intend to do whether I live one year or twenty.

In the following parable, I don't think Christ was just talking about money. Wealth can be defined in many ways. I think the more important point of the parable is that only when we are willing to give up *everything* to follow Him, will we understand and experience the kind of peace He bestows on us.

Parable of Rich Man

When Jesus heard this, He said to him, "You still lack one thing. Sell everything you have and give to the poor, and you will have treasure in heaven. Then come, follow me." When he heard this, he became very sad, because he was a man of great wealth. Jesus looked at him and said, "How hard it is for the rich to enter the kingdom of God! Indeed, it is easier for a camel to go through the eye of a needle than for a rich man to enter the kingdom of God." Those who heard this asked, "Who then can be saved?" Jesus replied, What is impossible with men is possible with God." Peter said to him, "We have left all we had to follow you!" "I tell you the truth," Jesus said to them, "no one who has left home or wife or brothers or parents or children for the sake of the kingdom of God will fail to receive many times as much in this age and, in the age to come, eternal life."
Luke 18:23-30

I once heard an African man speak about his time in the United States as a student. As he was returning home, he was asked what he thought about Americans. His answer prompted me to think of this parable. He said that he felt sorry for Americans because they have so much yet so little. In countries where poverty reigns, not always, but often, faith abounds because people aren't slaves to their "stuff." This allows them the freedom to cling to God, rather than their belongings like the young man in Christ's story.

At any rate, when people insist on praying for a specific outcome, I've always believed that they are more concerned with what *they* want than what God wants. It illustrates a certain lack of trust that God knows what's best. It occurred to me that in situations such as mine, God wisely gives us the responsibility of praying because He knows our desperate need to be 'DOING' something. Despite our name, human 'BEINGS' have a difficult time just 'being' still and knowing that He is God. As I expect God intended, prayers comfort those praying, not necessarily those for whom they pray. If we truly trusted God, we could rest in the knowledge that he knows better than anyone what's best for us, and we would allow Him that freedom without nagging. If my own children repeatedly ask me for something I have already answered with a negative, they get punished. I've learned from experience that if they don't like the answer, they are going to like the reason even less, so I don't engage in a discussion. It is a no-win situation and just prolongs the inevitable. "Because I said so" will suffice, and I have to think that at times God must feel the same. Here, too, is human audacity at its worst. If you are tempted to ask why God didn't answer your prayers, ask yourself this question. Why do we think we deserve an explanation? God doesn't need to explain His decisions, but He has revealed His *character* so that we can trust Him without needing to know "Why?" I know *who* He is, so I gladly accept His parental "Because I said so." How silly we are to consider ourselves God's peers. We wouldn't be able to understand even if He chose to offer an explanation – any more than a toddler understands limits imposed by his parents.

For my thoughts are not your thoughts,
neither are your ways my ways, declares the Lord.
As the heavens are higher than the earth,
so are my ways higher than your ways
and my thoughts than your thoughts.
Isaiah 55:8-9

But who are you, O man, to talk back to God?
"Shall what is formed say to him who formed it,
'Why did you make me like this?' "
Does not the potter have the right to make out of the same lump of
clay some pottery for noble purposes and some for common use?
Romans 9:20-21

Oh, the depth of the riches of the wisdom and knowledge of God!
How unsearchable his judgments,
and his paths beyond tracing out!
Who has known the mind of the Lord?
Or who has been his counselor?'
Who has ever given to God,
that God should repay him?'
For from him and through him and to him are all things.
To him be the glory forever! Amen.
Romans 11:33-36

It never fails to amaze me how humans are always trying to wrestle with God for power and control. I've spent my life trying to overcome a need to control. Just a note of caution here – when you ask God for help in an area in which you struggle, you can bet He will put you in situations where you can practice during your recovery. How do you think I ended up in my current predicament?

Regardless, once you achieve the peace that Jesus tried to impart during His short life, it makes any situation less frightening and life more enjoyable. Christ isn't guaranteeing a peaceful life. He is offering peace amidst life, which is anything but peaceful.

I have told you these things so that in me you have peace.
In this world you will have trouble.
John 16:33a

Peace I leave with you; my peace I give you.
I do not give to you as the world gives.
Do not let your hearts be troubled and do not be afraid.
John 14:27

Whenever Christ needed regenerating or faced difficult decisions, temptation, or danger, He didn't send out a call to arms. He slipped away and enjoyed some quiet time with God, which is exactly my approach.

But Jesus often withdrew to lonely places and prayed.
Luke 5:16

After he had dismissed them,
he went up on a mountainside by himself to pray.
When evening came, he was there alone.
Matthew 14:23

When you pray, go into your room,
close the door and pray to your Father, who is unseen.
Then your Father,
who sees what is done in secret, will reward you.
And when you pray,
do not keep on babbling like pagans,
for they think they will be
heard because of their many words.
Do not be like them,
for your Father knows what you need before you ask him.
Matthew 6:8

Very early in the morning,
while it was still dark, Jesus got up,
left the house and went off to a solitary place,
where he prayed.
Mark 1:35

The most obvious problem with the logic that you can manipulate or bargain with God through prayer is that it implies that when He doesn't answer in the way you expect, it must mean that you didn't pray hard enough or have enough people praying for you. Life is not a popularity contest, and God doesn't play favorites. At least not the God I know. He takes care of everyone equally – the ones clambering for attention as well as the ones sitting quietly at His feet. Keep in mind, sometimes the most effective way to get someone's attention *is* to whisper because they have to draw nearer to hear you. God knows my name. He doesn't need to be reminded to take care of me.

> *Are not two sparrows sold for a penny?*
> *Yet not one of them will fall to the ground*
> *apart from the will of your Father.*
> *And even the very hairs of your head are all numbered.*
> *So don't be afraid;*
> *you are worth more than many sparrows.*
> *Matthew 10:29-31*

The true value of prayer is that it is an expression of our love for God and each other, and it is this love that comforts us and pleases God. God doesn't instruct us to pray always because He needs to be reminded of our needs. It's because *we* need to be reminded of His presence and sovereignty; which, in turn, fills us with His comfort and peace.

In addition, it is clear from the following passage that Jesus could see that His disciples weren't getting it. If His closest friends couldn't feel peaceful with Him right there beside them, how can we? Only with His help, of course, and *a lot of prayer.*

> *Then he got into the boat and his disciples followed him. Without warning, a furious storm came up on the lake, so that the waves swept over the boat. But Jesus was sleeping. The disciples went and woke him, saying, 'Lord, save us! We're going to drown!' He replied, 'You of little faith, why are you so afraid?' Then he*

*got up and rebuked the winds and the waves, and it
was completely calm. The men were amazed and asked,
'What kind of man is this? Even the winds and the
waves obey him!'*

Matthew 8:23-27

Yet, this is exactly the kind of peace I feel. The peace that
enables me to sleep amidst a raging storm with no doubt
that Jesus will take care of me, whether it means bringing
me home or curing my illness. Praying is an effort to capture
this peace, to offer and receive comfort, to afford us the
feeling that we are "doing" something when really (as usual)
it is God's way of comforting us and offering us shelter in
a storm. It forces us into stillness where we can feel His
calming, restorative peace and power. As I mentioned earlier,
we as humans love to feel that we are in control or that we
can help God do a better job. We suffer from the delusion
that we are better equipped to know when and on whom He
should perform a miracle.

The biggest problem I see with this mentality is the
question of how to respond to the grieving parent of a
young child or any number of seemingly senseless tragedies.
Did their child die because there weren't enough prayers or
just not enough of the right ones? Were those praying not
convincing enough? I don't think so. The fact is, we don't
have the answers. Some things will remain a mystery until we
arrive in Heaven with our long list of 'whys.' As an example
of faith, my sister uses Henslowe in *Shakespeare in Love* who,
when describing the theatre business could be explaining life
itself.

Henslowe:	*Allow me to explain about the theatre business. The natural condition is one of insurmountable obstacles on the road to imminent disaster.*
Fennyman:	*So what do we do?*
Henslowe:	*Nothing. Strangely enough, it all turns out well.*
Fennyman:	*How?*
Henslowe:	*I don't know. It's a mystery.*

I couldn't agree more.

Clearly, their exchange is an oversimplification. Henslowe doesn't mean *nothing* literally anymore than God expects us to coast through life doing *nothing*. All we can do is use the talents and resources God has given us to the best of our ability while trusting Him to write the final act.

Throughout my life when traveling rough terrain, I was tempted to think God wasn't listening. Sometimes it wasn't until years later that I could see how much I had gained, despite the pain I felt at the time. Only in hindsight could I recognize God's handiwork. Does anybody willingly enter the fire for their own good? A few, I suppose, but not many and certainly not me. Self-preservation is a powerful instinct. All I know is that, as a child of God, He alone determines my future. I don't need to know what it is because, frankly, it would ruin the adventure. However, I do know "that in all things God works for the good of those who love him, who have been called according to his purpose." (Romans 8:28)

Now, with all I've said about prayer, I still rely on some of the formal prayers I learned as a youngster which truly embody that for which I pray. I leave you with two of my favorites.

The Serenity Prayer
Reinhold Niebuhr, 1934

God grant me the serenity
To accept the things I cannot change;
Courage to change the things I can;
And wisdom to know the difference.

Living one day at a time,
Enjoying one moment at a time
Accepting hardships as the pathway to peace,
Taking, as Jesus did,
This sinful world as it is,
Not as I would have it,
Trusting that You will make all things right,
If I surrender to Your will,
So that I may be reasonably happy in this life,
And supremely happy with You forever in the next.
Amen

Peace Prayer of St. Francis of Assisi

Lord, make me an instrument of your peace;
where there is hatred, let me sow love;
when there is injury, pardon;
where there is doubt, faith;
where there is despair, hope;
where there is darkness, light;
and where there is sadness, joy.
Grant that I may not so much seek
to be consoled as to console;
to be understood, as to understand,
to be loved as to love;
for it is in giving that we receive,
it is in pardoning that we are pardoned,
and it is in dying that we are born to eternal life.

Suffering Servant

She came to him and asked,
"Lord, don't you care that my sister
has left me to do the work by myself?
Tell her to help me!"
Luke 10:40b

Why do people describe those who die as brave, courageous, or sometimes even inspiring? You'd think we actually had a choice in the matter. I suppose we do in that we choose how we face death the same way we choose how we face life: fearfully or joyfully. Why should we expect to be any different in death than we are in life? Let me tell you something. Dying is easy; it's the living that's a killer. The only option available to us is how we decide to do both, and it is that decision that defines us.

For me dying fulfilled a role I had been practicing for all my life – martyr. Suffering from a deeply ingrained martyr syndrome, I was well prepared for my new role as "Cancer Lady." Couldn't God have just settled for a "Church Lady" position? Though I had to admit, I didn't have much training in that area. I think all Catholics have a bit of the martyr in them because, as children, they were our idols. One of my fellow campers at Camp Marydell, an all-girl's, Catholic sleep away camp run by the Sisters of Our Lady of Christian Doctrine, remembers how

> ...the sisters regaled us wide-eyed innocents around the campfire with tales of different martyrs including St. Lawrence and how he was *slowly roasted to death*. Still, he had the good humor to tell his tormentors, 'Turn me over - I'm not done on this side!' Wow! Who needs ghost stories when Butler's *Lives of the Saints* provided such great tales?

Make no mistake, being a Christian martyr was equivalent to winning *American Idol*, only the reward was death. My patron saint is Joan of Arc. I had some big shoes to fill.

Having a flare for the dramatic also qualified me for my final role. I'm one of those people who would sit and torture myself after a romantic breakup by listening to every sad song I could find about lost love and women scorned. I cried the pain out. This was no different. It's actually quite an effective coping mechanism. Like all of God's creations, tears serve a valuable purpose. Releasing all those tears had a calming, cleansing effect and allowed me to face the process of dying with more composure than I felt. These episodes were usually done in solitude but occasionally I would share my tears with those I knew would allow me the freedom to cry without telling me it was going to be okay when we both knew it wasn't – at least not by worldly standards. Sometimes you just need someone to cry with or a shoulder to cry on.

Anyway, our family thrives on melodrama. There are too many stories to tell (probably another book there), but those who know me are aware of some of our most famous scenes: the Peep-Stomping incident, the Shoebox Note, my temper tantrum Hannah broadcast on iChat, or just my daily cry, "Stop looking at me." Some are funny – usually after a respectable amount of time has passed to gain perspective and recognize their humor. Some aren't so funny, but they all make for an Oscar-worthy reality show. You just can't make this stuff up.

My current situation was merely the final scene of a life-long soap opera. How did I want to play this one out? Ali McGraw style in *Love Story?* Debra Winger in *Terms of Endearment?* Or maybe Barbara Hershey in *Beaches?* No, I decided to do it in my own style, the way I lived my life: with humor, grit, and hopefully, a certain panache. Maybe I'll leave instructions to play *I Did It My Way* at my service along with all the other tear jerkers with which I'd been torturing myself.

I can't recall the exact circumstances, but sometime after the first surgery, my teenage daughter blurted out, "Could you stop with the cancer thing? You just want everyone to feel sorry for you." I don't usually take her criticisms to heart because I learned long ago I was a constant source of embarrassment to my children. What parent isn't? I relish my role and take my job of "ruining her life" quite seriously. I've learned an interesting fact being a parent. Ruining someone's life is not a one-time event. It is a long, arduous process. My standard reply to my children's often-heard lament "You're Ruining My Life" is a heavy sigh and the retort, "I thought I did that last week. How much longer is this going to take? I'm exhausted." The question I raise is just how many times and in how many different ways can you ruin someone's life? Apparently, the opportunities are endless. I've discovered it doesn't take much effort. Some days, simply being alive is sufficient.

With all that said, her comment made me pause and think. Was she on to something? I didn't think so, but then again I did have a genetic predisposition towards martyrdom. Reluctantly, I had to admit to pulling out the cancer card on a few occasions. You just have to be careful not to abuse it. I decided to stick with my original strategy of ignoring the sometimes outrageous comments teenagers blurt out but with the caveat of monitoring myself for any sign of validity in her statement.

Kitty Slattery states in her tender memoir, *Lost and Found*, that "In God's economy, nothing in life goes to waste." Cancer is no exception. I just needed to determine what God wanted me to do with mine other than looking for sympathy, as my daughter accused. My father wrote something to me that I truly believe: "Whatever happens, I know we will all be blessed by it." My new assignment was to learn what blessing God wanted me to reveal to others. No easy feat considering I wasn't sure just how much time I had. It would be so much easier if God still spoke audibly to us as in the Old Testament. Nevertheless, I was confident that if He wanted something done, He would make sure I got the message one way or another.

The trouble with trying to listen to God is that my own ideas keep getting in the way. "Maybe He wants me to do this or maybe that," and so on. The key to hearing Him is emptying your mind of the nonsense to make room for His substance. That's it. I didn't have to complicate things or over think them. It was probably something simple, as are most of His messages. He really has to dumb everything down for us because we are so dense. We can take the simplest message and convolute it to the point of distortion. Perhaps God just wanted me to assure everyone once again, "Do not be afraid," or maybe He wanted to use me as a reminder that we should "be joyful always; pray continually; give thanks in **all** circumstances, for this is God's will for you in Christ Jesus." (1 Thessalonians 5:16-18)

If we are truly meant to be Christ-like, then we are all born to die. What happens in between determines what happens afterward. Remember, Christ died a young man. I often wondered why Jesus couldn't stay longer. Who knows? I suppose God thought His work was finished. The fact is, God alone determines the how, where, when, and why of our departure. He just doesn't share that knowledge with us. It all comes down to trust. Once you establish that trust, the fear dissipates and is replaced by an inexplicable joy.

Preparing to die is a busy affair. There are just too many things I wanted to say and do before leaving. Not traveling to distant places or seeing amazing sights like Jack Nicholson and Morgan Freeman in *The Bucket List*, but getting the house in order. I know, that's sick; but oddly enough, other than letters to my family, my main concern was getting everything in its place to make things easier after I left. I am not a neat freak. It wasn't neatness I was working toward but organization. After all, my husband and children weren't going to be able to call me on my cell phone to ask where the football pants were (as if I were the last one to wear them) or who was supposed to be where and when. I looked at it like writing a job description for my replacement.

It was similar to the nesting instinct that consumed me during pregnancy, and it was no different than what I go through preparing to leave even for one day. Notes and schedules for each child along with where to find essential items that for some reason no one else can seem to locate. We were in the middle of a construction job when the cancer resurfaced, so this was not the ordinary getting things in order. This was disorder of monstrous proportions. But, I thought, if God could create the world out of chaos in seven days, certainly he could handle this small mess. I relay the story as a reminder of God's faithfulness because I believe it was His reminder to me.

As with most construction projects, the chances of completing on schedule are remote. Once we discovered that I was either going to be having surgery or beginning chemo, the contractor turned up the heat. Anyone who has lived through construction will recognize the divine intervention that enabled the job to be completed so quickly. It wasn't that it was without problems, but that each glitch was solved quickly and with an even better result, as if someone was purposely redirecting us. Every detail fell into place beautifully and perfectly. It was similar to God instructing Noah how to build the ark down to the smallest detail. Throughout the Old Testament God's attention to detail is evident in His care of the Israelites. Come to think of it, any project I've done that has come out well, I've felt that same divine inspiration and intervention guiding and directing my every step – almost as if God was painting a canvas and just using me (and the contractor and his crew of subs) as His brushes. The best part about it is that everyone arrived happy, no one got flustered despite a hiccup here and there, and they all worked together skillfully and smoothly even though there were times when they were tripping over each other, eager to help finish before my surgery.

I won't bore you with every detail, but can't resist sharing a couple. On a lark I decided to call a decorative painter I had worked with some years back. I was in Texas at the time on my own sort of sabbatical. Dialing his cell phone intending to leave a message, I was surprised when a groggy Robert answered sleepily. Even though it was early afternoon, I apologized for waking him up. He informed me that he was in India, and it was the middle of the night. I asked if he was still painting, and He told me he would be back from his pilgrimage in three months and would call me then. True to his word, he called in early October. I briefly described the project, and we made an appointment for him to come take a look. When he arrived, I asked him about his journey, and he told me how weird it was that I had reached him. He was in some rural village, woke up in the middle of the night and was trying to determine the time. As there were no clocks in sight, he decided to plug in his cell phone. As soon as he plugged it in, my call came in, we had our brief conversation, he checked the time, then unplugged the phone. He said it was the only time he even bothered to plug it in as there was usually no service. Anyway, Robert made a sample the previous night and laid it out on the table. It was perfect. Remember, he hadn't seen the space yet. The colors matched the walls and mirrored the counter and backsplash. It was uncanny. Even Robert was stunned. With that settled, we had little to discuss except price. When I presented his quote to my husband, he asked, "Do we really need Michelangelo to do the ceiling of this little space?" Don't argue with the divine, I chided. Despite Bob's hesitation, Robert started a week later.

I remained in awe of the perfection of the colors and treatment he chose. It was better than I had imagined. As I drove through town admiring God's palette of fall foliage, I laughed to myself. If He could create this, why was I always surprised by His ability to design beauty?

There were other God moments too. I got a call unexpectedly in October from the furniture store to let me know my order had arrived six weeks early. They couldn't understand it, and assured me it was very unusual. Could I take delivery? Then, the next day the plumber came to install the faucet, which we discovered didn't fit. I ran out to get a larger one. Just finding a salesperson in Klaff's is equivalent to parting the Red Sea so when I was helped immediately, I knew it was a good sign. Unfortunately, she informed me they did not keep any of the size I needed in stock. "Humor me," I begged. "Could you just check?" Sure enough, they had one in stock. The clerk didn't believe it and insisted the computer must be wrong. She called the warehouse where they produced exactly what I needed. Somehow, I wasn't surprised. You might think it a stretch to think that God was behind these things. Some might say God is too big to get involved in such trivia. I think just the opposite. God is too big *not* to get involved. If there is one thing I've learned in my spiritual journey, it's that God is found in the details.

In Joshua 4 God instructs him to build memory stones as a reminder of His promise to always be with the Israelites and care for them. Strange as it may seem, my completed rooms were God's reminder to me of how He provides for me in my time of need.

He (Joshua) said to the Israelites, "In the future when your descendants ask their fathers, 'What do these stones mean?' tell them, 'Israel crossed the Jordan on dry ground.' For the LORD your God dried up the Jordan before you until you had crossed over. The LORD your God did to the Jordan just what he had done to the Red Sea when he dried it up before us until we had crossed over. He did this so that all the peoples of the earth might know that the hand of the Lord is powerful and so that you might always fear the Lord your God."

Joshua 4:21-24

This wasn't the first time God took over a project for me when He needed me elsewhere. When God has a job for you, He will pick up the slack and tend to the minutiae of your life – quite nicely, I might add. It's a shame we don't allow Him that freedom more often. Once again, God had shown me His trustworthiness so that I could be comforted in the knowledge that He was watching over me and my family. How could I forget or dismiss the fact that my husband and children were His children first, and He could and would care for them just fine without my help. These rooms were God's memory stones erected as a testimony to His benevolent care for us.

You might be wondering what happened to my martyr topic, which is exactly where I found myself by this point. It is tough to be a suffering servant when you are being cared for so lovingly. When you learn to recognize God's hand in your life, it is impossible to feel like a martyr. Quite the opposite, you can't do enough for Him, and it doesn't feel like work or suffering. Sometimes it's not easy; but given the right attitude, you can find joy in any assignment from God. He may not choose to cure my cancer, but He certainly did a fine job of curing my martyr syndrome. Move over Mary, I'm laying down my cross to rest at Jesus' feet.

> *As Jesus and his disciples were on their way, He came to a village where a woman named Martha opened her home to Him. She had a sister called Mary, who sat at the Lord's feet listening to what He said. But Martha was distracted by all the preparations that had to be made. She came to Him and asked, 'Lord, don't you care that my sister has left me to do the work by myself? Tell her to help me!' 'Martha, Martha,' the Lord answered, 'you are worried and upset about many things, but only one thing is needed. Mary has chosen what is better, and it will not be taken away from her.'*
> *Luke 10:38-42*

No Fair!

Yet you say, 'The way of the Lord is not fair.'
Hear now, O house of Israel,
is it not My way which is fair,
and your ways which are not fair?
Ezekiel 18:25
New King James Version

I wish I had a dime for every time I heard my kids declare, "That's not fair." I'd be richer still if I'd had a dime for every time I made that same declaration as a child and well into adulthood. As a child, I may have *thought* life was unfair. With maturity, it became fact. LIFE'S NOT FAIR. Good thing too, I tell my children; because if life was fair, you'd have a lot less.

What then shall we say? Is God unjust? Not at all!
For he says to Moses,
'I will have mercy on whom I have mercy,
and I will have compassion on whom I have compassion.'
Romans 9:14-15

I no longer feel cheated by the inequities of life. I feel guilty for having so much. "Why me?" is something I ask when I look at all my blessings. Why should I be so blessed while so many struggle to merely survive? Once you arrive at that attitude of gratitude, your life becomes one long thank you as you use your gifts to enhance the lives of others and your suffering to glorify God.

But what about your cancer? I've often been asked, "Don't you ever wonder 'Why me?'" On the contrary, my response is "Why not me?" When God was showering me with blessings, it didn't occur to me to respond, "Why me? No more please. Give it to someone else." Well, I don't look at cancer any differently. Strange as it seems, I view my illness as yet another one of God's blessings, and one I gladly accept because I can use it to glorify Him.

When people ask me if I suffer from self pity or a 'Why me?' attitude, I am reminded of a line adults used frequently when I was growing up. "You want something to cry about? I'll give you something to cry about." It was usually followed with a whack up the side of your head. The nuns were particularly fond of this method. Even the dullest kid learned quickly, whining wasn't worth it.

Like any parent, God too must get tired of listening to His children whine and be tempted to give us a good whack now and again. He may use that tact on occasion, but for the most part our Father is amazingly patient with all our complaining. Studying Exodus would be a perfect example. First, He sends the Israelites Moses, and they complain because Moses is causing problems for them with the Pharaoh. Then God leads them out of Egypt and delivers them from their enemies by parting the Red Sea. God provides their freedom, yet still they complain. They groaned because they were hungry, so God provided food. They cried out in thirst, so God provided water. The list goes on and on.

If only we had died by the Lord's hand in Egypt!
There we sat around pots of meat
and ate all the food we wanted,
but you have brought us out into this desert
to starve this entire assembly to death.
Exodus 16:3

You will know that it was the Lord
when he gives you meat to eat in the evening
and all the bread you want in the morning,
because he has heard your grumbling against him.
Exodus 16:8

Why did you bring us up out of Egypt to make us and our children
and livestock die of thirst?'
Then Moses cried out to the Lord,
'What am I to do with these people?
They are almost ready to stone me.'
Exodus 17:3-4

In any event, when I first learned I had cancer, it never occurred to me to ask "Why me?" In fact, my response was "Why not me?" We are surrounded by people suffering from cancer in epidemic proportions. There were a lot of people worse off than me. Why should I expect to be spared? Did my Christianity guarantee a long and healthy life? Hardly.

Even so, I have to be honest. Following the second surgery, when I started experiencing the normal symptoms of menopause (hot flashes, irritability, depression, insomnia, etc.), it was the only time I actually caved and cried, "If I'm going to die anyway, is this really necessary?" Apparently it was, and shame on me for asking. A crisis like cancer I could handle readily with God's help; however, a normal menopause managed to throw me into a funk. Dare I say it? I felt like He owed me. "I'm going along with your plan, God, couldn't you just cut me some slack on this?" Have I mentioned before that I am a slow learner?

When considering the ubiquitous question of why, the best answer I've ever heard was while watching C. S. Lewis's *Prince Caspian* recently with my son. In the closing scene, Aslan offers the Telmarines a prosperous future by returning to the land of their birth. "Your future in that world shall be good." Still, only a few accept Aslan's proposal while most stubbornly refuse, fearful and suspicious despite Aslan's assurances of safety. Reepicheep, the valiant mouse, steps forward and volunteers to lead by example and enter the portal. However, it is the children that ultimately assume that role. Peter announces, "Come on, we'll go. Our time's up. After all, we're not really needed here anymore." Susan agrees and adds the stunning truth, "We're not coming back." In response to the younger sister's anguished cry to Aslan, "*But why?* Did they do something wrong?" Aslan responds,

> Quite the opposite, dear one, but all things have their time. Your brother and sister have learned what they can from this world. Now, it's time for them to live in their own.[7]

I believe God would like our response to be similar to Peter's when he comforts his sister, "It's alright, Lu. It's not how I thought it would be, but it's alright. One day you'll see too."[7] We will all find our answers eventually; but until that time, I trust God enough to know it's going to be okay, despite all appearances to the contrary.

Michael Crawford sings a Christmas song as the voice of Joseph asking God "Why me?" not in a whining manner, but in awe and wonder at being chosen to parent God's son. He sings, "Why me? I'm just a simple man of trade. Why her? She's just an ordinary girl?" In carpenter's terminology, Joseph nailed it. It was specifically for their simplicity that they were chosen. A missionary once told me if you don't think you're qualified, then you're just the person God's looking for. This way there is no confusion as to who gets the glory.

Needless to say, Joseph and Mary were two people who clearly had something to whine about. Mary finds herself pregnant with no husband. Joseph learns that his betrothed is with child and is expected to believe the father is God. Their circumstances were frightening, but here they were marveling at the extraordinary honor and responsibility they had been given. My prayer is that if I am tempted to ask "Why me," may it be asked with the same reverence, and that I be granted the courage to accept any assignment God chooses to give me no matter how difficult it may appear at first.

'I am the Lord's servant,' Mary answered.
'May it be to me as you have said.'
Luke 1:38

When Joseph woke up,
he did what the angel of the Lord had commanded him
and took Mary home as his wife.
Matthew 1:24

Love on the Rocks

We also rejoice in our sufferings,
because we know that suffering produces perseverance;
perseverance, character; and character, hope.
And hope does not disappoint us,
because God has poured out his love
into our hearts by the Holy Spirit, whom he has given us.
Romans 5:3-5

Judging from the title, those who know me might suspect that I am about to reveal my husband's secret for serving a "perfect" Manhattan. I hate to disappoint you, but I couldn't think of a way to work that into a devotional book (or maybe I just did). The quote I chose reveals that the kind of rocks to which I refer won't be found in a cocktail. You don't have to be a drinker to appreciate life on the rocks. It's the only way it's served. Personally, I like mine straight up, but we don't always get that option. In Romans 5:3-5, Paul is clear about his view on suffering, but knowing it is for our own good doesn't necessarily make it any easier to swallow for the average person, and rejoicing in it is even harder. Aesop's fable about a desperate crow is a good example of the way suffering has worked in my life.

The Crow and the Pitcher

A crow, half-dead with thirst, came upon a pitcher which had once been full of water; but when the crow put its beak into the mouth of the pitcher he found that only very little water was left in it, and that he could not reach far enough down to get at it. He tried, and he tried, but at last had to give up in despair. Then a thought came to him, and he took a pebble and dropped it into the pitcher. Then he took another pebble and dropped that into the pitcher. Then he took another pebble and dropped that into the pitcher. Then he took another pebble and dropped that into the pitcher. Then he took another pebble and dropped that into the pitcher. Then he took another pebble and dropped that into the pitcher. At last, at last, he saw the water mount up near him, and after casting in a few more pebbles he was able to quench his thirst and save his life.

God pours a portion of His liquid love into each of us. However, for some of us it is the pebbles that get dropped in later that bring His presence bubbling up to the surface, quenching our thirst and restoring our soul. Without those pebbles we may never have had the ability or the desire to drink from His living water and recognize the presence and power of His saving grace within us.

Does this mean we don't get bogged down by the weight of our pebbles? Quite the contrary. I think they are designed to weigh us down, to bring us to our knees. It is there that most of us recognize our own inability to bear their weight alone, nor is that God's intention. When we feel overwhelmed by our burdens, whatever their cause, God is waiting to lighten our load, to offer us a lifespring of His grace, mercy, and love which will sustain us and strengthen us, whatever our circumstances. Like the persistent crow, He will never give up until our thirst for Him is satisfied.

If anyone is thirsty, let him come to me and drink.
Whoever believes in me, as the Scripture has said,
streams of living water will flow from within him.
John 7:37b-38

For the Lamb at the center of the throne will be their shepherd;
He will lead them to springs of living water.
And God will wipe away every tear from their eyes.
Revelation 7:17

Thank you, Lord, for being persistent with me, for caring enough to keep sending me pebbles so that I could know you and love you. Thank you for loving me too much to leave me as I was. Thank you for serving up the only cocktail I'll ever need. May your joy and strength help me carry my rocks in a way that will glorify you. Help me honor you in all I do. Amen.

Bob's Perfect Manhattan

1 part Sweet Vermouth (Noilly Prat)
1 part Dry Vermouth (Noilly Prat)
4 parts Jack Daniels (ratio should be at least 2:1
    but can go 3:1 for a dryer drink)
Dash of Angostura Bitters
Drop of Cherry Juice

Chill martini glasses first.
Mix ingredients in cocktail shaker with lots of ice.
Shake thoroughly (the colder, the better)
Pour into glasses, garnish with cherry and orange slice.
Drink cautiously and sparingly.

Whatever!

Finally, brothers, whatever is true,
whatever is noble, whatever is right,
whatever is pure, whatever is lovely,
whatever is admirable —
if anything is excellent or praiseworthy —
think about such things.
Whatever you have learned or received or heard from me,
or seen in me — put it into practice.
And the God of peace will be with you.
Phillipians 4:8-9

Anyone with children above the age of ten will recognize the universal expression "whatever." I can't recall what our generation's equivalent was, but I'm sure my mother could. Well, I am guilty of using the same expression with my heavenly Father, but not quite with the same attitude.

In the Bible we are taught that whatever occupies your mind determines the kind of person you become. If you choose to dwell on all the suffering and misery in the world, you will be tempted to fall into the pit of despair. If you worry excessively about things you cannot control, you will become a neurotic insomniac. If you brood over all the things wrong in your life, you will feel victimized. If you are consumed with vengeance, you will become bitter and angry.

On the other hand, if you make a choice to reflect on God's goodness and faithfulness despite your circumstances, He promises peace; and then you too will be able to claim that you "have learned to be content *whatever* the circumstances." (Philippians 4:11)

Considering this, Paul's instruction to the Phillipians makes perfect sense. They had a hard life. They were facing persecution and death for their beliefs. It would have been easy for them to succumb to self-pity, or to cry out in frustration that the cost for their faith was too high. Still, Paul encouraged them to master their thoughts by focusing on God's promises and to concentrate on God's goodness rather their own difficulties.

> *Do not conform any longer to the pattern of this world,*
> *but be transformed by the renewing of your mind.*
> *Romans 12:2*

The same can be said for many Christians today. We all have suffering of some kind. It is part of life. Having a terminal illness doesn't make one unique. There are a lot worse things than death. Even so, dealing with a terminal illness can be all-consuming, as can any form of suffering. My own mortality is never far from my mind. It takes incredible discipline and determination to avoid drowning in self-pity or sadness when I think of not growing old with my husband or never holding my grandchildren. I use Paul's words as a constant reminder to focus on the abundance of God's blessings I've been given. I refuse to allow this disease to become who I am because my identity is defined by my life, not my death, by my Christianity not my illness. I want the "Big C" in my life to be Christ not cancer.

Don't misunderstand me. This is not always easy. Joni Eareckson Tada puts it like this,

> When I speak of having faith in God during our times of suffering and crises, I am not talking about an emotion. Trusting God is not necessarily having trustful feelings. It is an act of the will. Because essentially, trusting God is reasoning with yourself to act upon what you know in your head to be true, even though you do not feel like it is true.[8]

We all have moments of weakness (which Satan waits and watches for) where we are tempted to lose trust in God or to think He has forsaken us. Isn't that what Jesus cried from the cross? This is why Ms. Eareckson Tada suggests that at times "it is an act of will." It's like trying to forgive someone or love a difficult person. You make the choice to forgive or love in your head long before it actually happens in your heart.

Studying the Bible reminds me of God's promises, trustworthiness, mercy, benevolence, and above all, His incredible love for us. These are the things I meditate on. And when I do, I can say without attitude, "Whatever, God, thy will be done."

The following song is what prompted this chapter because it addresses the absurdity of humans trying to advise God how we are going to help Him. Believe me, getting cancer would not have been on the top of my list. Based on His pleas in Gethsemane, I don't think crucifixion was Jesus' idea of a good plan either; but God doesn't have a Plan B, so wherever we find ourselves must be fulfilling some purpose that we can't see or possibly understand. The trick is not to ask "Why?" but to ask "What and How? What is it that you want me to do with this, God? How can I use this to glorify you?" I guarantee it will be in ways you would never have imagined, and often in areas in which you have no natural ability. This way, there will be no doubt as to who gets the glory. Life with God is anything but dull. It is a new adventure every day. We never know what's coming next, but we do know that He will equip us to deal with *whatever* with grace not attitude.

Whatever

by
Steven Curtis Chapman

I made a list, wrote down from A to Z
All the ways I thought that You could best use me
Told all my strengths and my abilities
I formed a plan it seemed to make good sense
I laid it out for You so sure You'd be convinced
I made my case, presented my defense
But then I read the letter that You sent me
It said that all You really want from me is just

Whatever, whatever You say
Whatever, I will obey
Whatever, Lord, have Your way
'Cause You are my God, whatever

So strike a match, set fire to the list
Of all my good intentions, all my preconceived ideas
I want to do Your will no matter what it is
Give me faith to follow where You lead me
Oh, Lord, give me the courage and the strength to do ...

I am not my own
I am Yours and Yours alone
You have bought me with Your blood
Lord, to You and You alone do I belong
And so whatever

The Cancer Card

No one says "NO" to a boy
with a terminal illness.
13, *Jason Robert Brown*

I've always looked forward to reaching old age because it earns you a certain liberty to speak your mind. I mentioned this to my sister one day who looked at me aghast, "There's more?" "Some things you just can't put in writing," I replied. "They'd never get past the editing stage." For my 51st birthday, my 12-year-old son gave me a home-made card that begins with this statement, "Official Old Age = Over 50." After listing some of the benefits of aging, he closes with "Another upside to being old is you can now say whatever you want, like grandpa does." It is not clear whether our internal edit button begins to malfunction after a certain age, or maybe we just choose not to exercise it, using senility as an excuse. Sadly, being an outspoken old lady may not be in the cards for me, so I decided that having a terminal illness should afford you similar freedoms as well. People tend to be a little more lenient once they realize you are bordering on senility or have cancer. In fact, sometimes I have to resist the temptation to exploit my condition (like using it as an excuse not to shovel this winter or to take in yet another Broadway show) or use it as a pretext to cover up questionable behavior or simply to get my own way.

For example, prior to my second surgery my family went out to dinner. I asked to stop at Baskin Robbins for an ice cream on our way home. My husband was suggesting we skip it when my daughter began singing *"No one says 'no' to a girl with a terminal illness"* from Jason Robert Brown's musical comedy *13* that we had seen recently. In the show a group of underage kids want to see an "R" rated movie, so they convince the boy with the terminal illness to ask his mother to buy them tickets, knowing she won't deny his request. You might think it callous, but we thought it was hilarious and oh so true. Needless to say, I got my ice cream – extra large!

I'll share another example. My husband keeps certain wines for special occasions in the basement. Much to his chagrin, I've been known to unwittingly pick out a "special occasion" wine to enjoy with friends. However, after I found out the cancer had returned, I proceeded to drink through his special occasion wines guilt free, and he never said a word, God bless him.

There is no question that you approach life differently when faced with a terminal illness. You take out the good dishes, cash in your airline miles, wear the nice outfit you've been saving for a special occasion, and develop a sort of black humor. My motto after my 51st birthday was "Old Trumps Dead Every Time!" You also enjoy every minute of every day with a new appreciation for the most precious gift of life. The little annoyances of daily life don't seem so irritating anymore, and daily dramas take on a little less importance. You develop a new mental barometer for measuring value. If I died tomorrow, how important would it be to have a clean house or all the laundry done? You'd be amazed how *un*important most things become when viewed in this light. The blessing with this new attitude is that you are left with so much more time to concentrate on things that do matter, though my family might disagree as to what those are. They might rate having clean underwear higher on the scale than I would.

The fact is, everyone will have a different answer to the question of importance. For me, it is relationships: my relationship with God, with others, and with myself. Those are what I think of in the middle of the night, not my next day's to-do list. After I'm gone, the house will still get cleaned and the laundry will still get done, but the relationships I leave behind will remain forever in the hearts of those I love in whatever state they happen to be in when I go. It would behoove me to ensure I leave them healthy and loving.

A person can have no better epitaph
than that which is inscribed in
the hearts of his friends.
Author Unknown

Christ came with a mission: to repair our broken relationship with God. Our salvation was His legacy to us.

For if, when we were God's enemies,
we were reconciled to him through the death of his Son,
how much more, having been reconciled,
shall we be saved through his life!
Romans 5:10

It would be my worst sin if I failed to accept His sacrifice on my behalf. With that in mind, what better way to spend my time (whether you have a terminal illness or not) than improving my relationship with Christ, which will inevitably improve any other relationship I'm in.

As far as the song goes, there is one "no" I've learned to accept, as difficult as that may seem. It is God's answer to my prayer for healing. For reasons beyond my understanding, it seems healing is not His answer for me, or at least not healing the way we understand it. However, I trust that He knows better than anyone what I need and why. In retrospect, every silent no I ever received from Heaven turned out to be exactly what I needed at the time, despite the pain it caused. Why should this be any different? So, while God may be the only one bold enough to say no to a girl with a terminal illness, I accept His will with grace and confidence that He will bring something good out of it, and we will all be blessed by it.

> *'For my thoughts are not your thoughts,*
> *neither are your ways my ways,' declares the Lord.*
> *'As the heavens are higher than the earth,*
> *so are my ways higher than your ways*
> *and my thoughts than your thoughts.'*
> *Isaiah 55:8-9*

> *You intended to harm me,*
> *but God intended it for good*
> *to accomplish what is now being done,*
> *the saving of many lives.*
> *Genesis 55:20*

I Love Lucy

Yes, life is heaven you see,
because I love Lucy,
Yes, I love Lucy,
and Lucy loves me!
Desi Arnaz

For reasons too numerous to mention, Lucy was added to a long list of nicknames I've acquired during the course of my life. For one, Lucy and Ricky were the code names my husband and I used when we began dating in the office. We didn't want anyone to know, so we would just leave messages to call Lucy or Ricky. At the office Christmas party we were given a homemade, heart-shaped ornament monogrammed with Lucy and Ricky that still hangs on our tree. I guess we didn't fool anybody.

Though I never had aspirations to be in show business, there is no denying some of my antics rivaled Lucy's escapades. My girlfriends and I have volunteered at places where we felt like Lucy and Ethel in the candy factory unable to keep up with the pace. Always, we laughed and sometimes ate our way through it.

Then there were the solo adventures. I remember one Father's Day when I had planned a barbecue for the family, then discovered I forgot to pick up the propane tank from the hardware store. Determined not to ruin Bob's day, and embarrassed by my own stupidity, I decided to scale the towering fence surrounding the lumberyard to retrieve the tank even while I worried about guard dogs. "Animals love me," I kept reassuring myself. Getting over wasn't bad, but climbing out with that heavy tank was no easy feat. I kept imagining how I would explain myself to the police if they happened by or if I would make it into the arrest notes of the local paper. Or worse yet, if I dropped this thing, would it explode? What a way to go. What would be the cause of death in my obituary?

Regardless, the big question looming before me now was how I was going to answer God when He says "Joanie, you've got some 'splaining to do." Perhaps I'll borrow Ralph Kramden's "Hamana-hamana-hamana-hamana."

All kidding aside, this was going to take some creative editing for sure. Didn't Adam and Eve already try that ploy? Maybe I'd get points for creativity to make up in the areas I was so sadly lacking. No, I don't think I'm going to be able to laugh my way out of this one.

The Sheep and the Goats

He will put the sheep on His right and the goats on His left. Then the King will say to those on his right, 'Come, you who are blessed by my Father; take your inheritance, the kingdom prepared for you since the creation of the world. For I was hungry and you gave me something to eat, I was thirsty and you gave me something to drink, I was a stranger and you invited me in, I needed clothes and you clothed me, I was sick and you looked after me, I was in prison and you came to visit me.'

Then the righteous will answer him, 'Lord, when did we see you hungry and feed you, or thirsty and give you something to drink? When did we see you a stranger and invite you in, or needing clothes and clothe you? When did we see you sick or in prison and go to visit you?'

The King will reply, 'I tell you the truth, whatever you did for one of the least of these brothers of mine, you did for me.'

Matthew 25:33-40

When It's All Been Said and Done is one of the masochistic songs I've been listening to and have pegged as the ultimate funeral tune because the lyrics sum up the end of anyone's life so succinctly.

> When it's all been said and done,
> There is just one thing that matters.
> Did I do my best to live for truth?
> Did I live my life for you?

I suppose that's the beauty of dying unexpectedly. You don't have to agonize over a lifetime of bad decisions. You don't have to second guess the way you've lived your life. As I reviewed my life and all the colossal blunders I'd made, my biggest disappointment was the time I wasted running from God. During a book group discussion recently, someone asked me what the biggest difference was in my life after developing a relationship with Christ. Without hesitation I answered, "Joy."

How sad that, for a better part of my life, I was pursuing joy in all the wrong places when it was imbedded in my heart before I was born. On the other hand, how blessed I was to have made that discovery before it was too late. The last eight years have been the happiest of my life, not because I wasn't experiencing any difficulties, but because life with God is fun. It is an adventure every day, another opportunity to bring His light into a world fraught with loneliness, fear, misery, and tragedy.

If we are all supposed to represent some character of God, I suppose mine would be His comic side. I guess you could say my job was to bring comic relief into a world that takes itself all too seriously – a Godly, "Lighten Up," for all those worriers. Maybe I could make a spoof of Lucy's "Vitameatavegamin" commercial to promote a spiritual health tonic guaranteed to introduce joy into your life. God knows, the world could use a daily dose.

Could it be that simple? Was I just supposed to remind people of the joy waiting for them through Jesus? I don't have to die to do that. But then again, Christ died for me, so how could I refuse this request? I may not be able to do it with style or eloquence, but I can say with confidence you will find delight in anything you do for Christ whether it be washing dishes, changing diapers, or battling cancer. When you get to know Jesus, He will give you a role in His show even though there is no guarantee you won't be written out of the script. Either way, once you've found Him, you've discovered your way home and love in its truest sense. Even Lucy can understand that point.

Yes, life is heaven you see,
because I love Lucy,
Yes, I love Lucy,
and Lucy loves me!

You bet I do!

The Burning Bush

There the angel of the LORD appeared
to him in flames of fire from within a bush.
Moses saw that though the bush was on fire it did not burn up.
Exodus 3:2

The Sunday before I went in for my second surgery, I was sitting at the kitchen table enjoying some quiet time gazing out at the beautiful fall foliage. One of my favorites is the fire bush: a relatively drab shrub most of the year, except for the fall when it screams a brilliant red, making all other foliage pale in comparison. I've been told that these bushes got their name because there are those that believe they were what Moses was looking at when he claimed to see God in the burning bush. Come on, I know Moses was old, but he wasn't an idiot. But then again, he did have trouble finding Israel and had everyone wandering around the desert for forty years.

Watching this spectacular display of beauty, it occurred to me that all these trees and shrubs "peak" just before dying or going dormant. Leaf peepers flock to New England to catch "the peak" with good reason. It is a cacophony of color, a work of art, God's own palette.

I began to wonder if the same holds true for people. Do we "peak" just before dying? My husband claims to have peaked in fourth grade, so I guess in his case my theory doesn't apply. Even so, the more I thought about it, the more I thought that these trees go through a peak every season, not just once. Maybe humans weren't so different after all. We all experience a variety of peaks during the course of our lives. People talk about leaving their careers on top whether they are corporate giants, athletes, teachers, actors, etc.

There are any number of areas in which we peak. For example, I've finally found a decent haircut, I've gotten as close to my ideal weight as possible for someone over 50, I can finally do a split after ten years of exercise class; but most importantly, at last I have felt the warmth of God's love permeating my entire being. While I don't believe any of us will truly peak spiritually until we are at home with the Lord, having cancer has brought me closer to God than I've ever been. It is for this reason that I view my illness as a gift, not a curse. I can go into surgery with complete confidence that, regardless of the outcome, my peak is still yet to come. Yes indeed, God makes "everything beautiful in His time." (Ecclesiastes 3:11a)

A Time for Everything

There is a time for everything,
and a season for every activity under heaven:
A time to be born and a time to die,
a time to plant and a time to uproot,
A time to kill and a time to heal,
a time to tear down and a time to build,
A time to weep and a time to laugh,
a time to mourn and a time to dance,
A time to scatter stones and a time to gather them,
a time to embrace and a time to refrain,
A time to search and a time to give up,
a time to keep and a time to throw away.
A time to tear and a time to mend,
a time to be silent and a time to speak,
A time to love and a time to hate,
a time for war and a time for peace.
Ecclesiastes 3:1-8

Act II: Surgery
Setting: Sloane Kettering, 11/4/08

I fear no harm, Lord,
for you are at my side!
Psalm 23:4

From the moment I arrived for check-in, it was clear the staff at Sloane Kettering remembered me as the first thing they gave me was the activity sheet for the week. Not a bad strategy. After a quick perusal, I knew when I needed to be up and around so as not to miss some of the highlights they had planned. Regrettably, unless they wheeled me from the recovery room right to bingo, I was going to miss it again.

When they deposited me into my friend John's (from last year) room, I knew I was not going to be disappointed. God had something planned for me, I was sure of it, which is the main reason I don't dislike my time in the hospital. God's presence is so palpable there. After they got me settled, I looked out the window and noticed a building with a huge "J" built into its chimney. One of the tips in the book, *Praying Through Cancer*, suggests visualizing something that reminds you of the Lord's protection and presence. I thought of a friend's son who calls Jesus the "J-man". Well, the "J-man" was keeping a close eye on me, and every time I looked out the window and saw that huge "J", I was reminded of God's promise,

> *'Never will I leave you; never will I forsake you.'*
> *So we say with confidence,*
> *'The Lord is my helper; I will not be afraid.'*
> Hebrews 13:5b-6a

When the night nurse came in, she took one look at me and exclaimed, "You again!" Another nurse was already in there encouraging me to get out of bed and walk a bit. Anita told her, "Don't you worry about her. She won't be in that bed long. She's Miss Busybody and will be all over this floor in no time."

As I said the last time, getting to know your neighbors is my favorite part of the hospital stay. From my first tentative lap around the floor, I scouted out potential walking companions. There was Herman who had been a bus driver in Brooklyn for 25 years. Then he moved to Louisiana and did landscaping for 25 years. He was probably in his late 70's and told me he met his 'girl' on the internet a few years ago. I guess you're never too old to try new things.

On a side trip for x-rays, I met a poet running the elevator. He appeared to be studying, so I asked if he was preparing for a test. He told me he was writing poetry. Would you share it with me? I inquired. He called it, *What Is True?* These are the kind of unexpected gems you stumble across regardless of where you find yourself. All it takes is an awareness of those around you and a desire to discover the beauty God has planted in every person. Sometimes, all you need to do is ask.

There are different kinds of gifts,
but the same Spirit.
1 Corinthians 12:4

When I got to radiology, I met a man whose name escapes me, probably because he kept comparing himself to an infamous porn star, Johnny Holmes. So I christened him Johnny H. He had to be in his late 80s, and assured me if he was twenty years younger, he would be romancing me. Given his reputation, I suppose I wouldn't have had a chance. He explained that he was quite the ladies man before he got sick. We passed the time discussing his numerous conquests over his lengthy romantic career. I was having such a good time; I was almost disappointed when they called my name. I left him trying to charm one of the nurses into his lap. Here is a man that took Christ's commandment to love thy neighbor to an entirely new level.

Then there was an elderly man I nicknamed Speedy, for the obvious reason. He raced around that floor like he was running for his life, which I suppose is probably not far from the truth. The funniest thing about Speedy is that he had no modesty. He'd just go gliding past with his gown flying loose and everything exposed. I was walking behind him giggling one day when the nurse stopped him and taped him shut with surgical tape. After a couple of days, I noticed he had figured out the double gown trick. As he dashed by me, he yelled over his shoulder. "No more free shows. I was getting everyone too excited." "Darn," I shouted after him. "Why do you think I've been following you around all week? You were the highlight of my day."

John was the one I walked with the most. He came calling a couple of times a day. He even accompanied me to the arts and craft room one day and sat and chatted with me while I made some hideously ugly stuffed animal that was suffering an identity crisis. We never could figure out whether it was a bear or a turkey. He was good company and promised to come take me to brunch at a local restaurant near my home when we got out. We'd feast on soup and Jell-O.

Dick was my immediate neighbor. The morning after surgery I stopped by to say hello. Not unlike last year, my new neighbor had something to teach me. Being Dick's neighbor was like riding shotgun with Job. This was his 11th operation since 2000, along with a stroke thrown in there at some point. In addition to whatever type of cancer his current surgery addressed, he also had shingles and stenosis in his hip. Yet, he was happy and surprisingly cheerful. He was on morphine, but even so. A few days into it, I asked him if it was his spirituality that allowed him to face his health challenges with such good humor. "No, it's my clients" he answered. He went on to say that he is usually working ½ hour after each operation, and he conducts business as usual from the hospital room. Everyone has a God. I suppose his was his work. Yet, I understood what God was showing me. This could be a long process, but I was comforted that I would have Him and not a slew of clients by my side all the way.

There was one man, I can't even recall his name, that I wanted to visit with, but just couldn't force myself to enter his room. It was obvious he was close to death. I never saw anyone visiting, and I just couldn't imagine what I could possibly say to him. Over the course of a week, I must have passed his room at least 50 times during my laps. Each time as I approached I would say, "If he's awake, I'll go in." or "If he's not on the phone, I'll go in." Secretly, I was relieved when he was either sleeping or otherwise occupied. Nevertheless, I could not stop thinking of him. On my last day there I was determined to enter his room. He was sleeping when I arrived. In the pocket of my robe was a guardian angel my daughter had given me before I left for the hospital. Quietly, I placed it on the table by his bed so he would see it when he awoke and know that he was not forgotten or alone. I have always regretted letting my fear prevent me from speaking to this man. Hopefully, that small reminder of God's presence offered a comfort that words could not.

We all knew what our ticket off the 15th floor was – some solid evidence that our digestive system was functioning properly. This was the only place I knew of where people were not reduced to embarrassment and giggles discussing passing gas or bowel movements. In fact, a chorus of gastric output would be a serenade for the health workers on the colorectal floor. Too bad there isn't an equivalent surgery or colon cleanser for the soul. Wouldn't it be great to just let go of all the gook clogging our spiritual system. I suppose that's the purpose of confession where our sins become spiritual sewerage, flushed away by God's mercy and grace.

I've suffered from more than one blockage in my spiritual life, and they can be just as painful as a physical one. Plus, there is no quick remedy. Make no mistake; surgery on the soul can be more painful than anything performed at Sloane Kettering. Much like the way my fellow inmates consulted skilled doctors to treat their ailments; we must also consult the original 'healer' to address our spiritual maladies.

Blessed is the man whom God corrects;
so do not despise the discipline of the Almighty.
For he wounds, but he also binds up;
He injures, but his hands also heal.
Job 5:17-18

Jesus said to them,
'It is not the healthy who need a doctor, but the sick.
I have not come to call the righteous, but sinners.'
Mark 2:17

God may not offer bingo or arts and crafts, but don't underestimate the healing power of a visit with him regardless of its duration. Some times may call for a lengthy stay, while other times brief but frequent visits suffice. When you consult a physician, you first need to explain your symptoms, then listen for his advice to determine the proper course of treatment. In a similar fashion, we need to do the same with God. Pour out your heart to him; then sit, rest, and wait for his peace and love to flow through you, cleansing your soul more thoroughly than a 10 oz. bottle of magnesium citrate.

This is what the LORD,
the God of your father David, says:
'I have heard your prayer and seen your tears;
I will heal you.'
2 Kings 20:5b

The thing about Jesus is that when He healed, he usually healed spiritual ailments first, then addressed the physical problems. He was more concerned with conditions of the heart than the body. While my surgeon is a talented man, unfortunately he couldn't heal my heart issues. For that I had to consult the Great Physician.

> *I said, 'O Lord, have mercy on me;*
> *Heal me, for I have sinned against you.'*
> *Psalm 41:4*

Back to my Sloane visit. When I woke up from surgery, I was astonished to learn from the surgeon that everything went much better than expected. After watching this tumor blossom from a raisin into a grapefruit in the span of just a couple of months, I thought for sure they were going to discover something horrific when they opened me up. I was mistaken. The horror was in my soul not my abdomen. "Another chapter for my *Green Banana* project," I thought. This one was going to be about not trying to front run God's plans. Did you ever hear the expression "Life is stranger than fiction?" Or here's another good one and certainly appropriate in my case. "Life is what happens while you're busy making plans." I was so busy preparing my dramatic exit; it didn't occur to me that perhaps God had made other arrangements. Actually, I did think about it quite a bit, and had decided maybe death *was* His plan for me. That's a slippery slope, trying to guess what God is up to. It's hard enough trying to decipher His voice when He wants to get your attention. And believe me, whatever He comes up with will be something you never considered. Once again, the laugh was on me. In current lingo, I woke up to a divine text message: JB – JK – JC. For those of you without teenagers, this translates to: *Joan Butman – Just Kidding – Jesus Christ.*

'For I know the plans I have for you,' declares the Lord,
'plans to prosper you and not to harm you,
plans to give you hope and a future.'
Jeremiah 29:11

Someone once told me that, as soon as you let go of your own plans and expectations, it gives God room to work. She went on to say that giving our will over to God allows His presence to take its proper place in our life. I just needed to get out of His way. All the funeral arrangements would have to be shelved for the present. God must not be finished with me quite yet. Nothing is wasted though, as those arrangements will be just as good whether I die tomorrow or after ten years of tomorrows. So, until my next visit, I just take it one day at a time being thankful for every tomorrow I'm granted. My only *plan* is to greet every morning in gratitude with the verse from Psalm 118:24 "This is the day the Lord has made; let us rejoice and be glad in it."

For Better or Worse

For this reason a man will leave his father and mother
and be united to his wife,
and the two will become one flesh.
So they are no longer two, but one.
Therefore what God has joined together,
let man not separate.
Matthew 19:5-6

Anyone who is married, and probably even those who aren't, will be familiar with those words. Like so many others, Bob and I shared them at our wedding ceremony in 1990. I can't speak for Bob, but a cancer diagnosis definitely seemed to fall on the worse side of the equation. Even still, it brought out the best in all of us. Funny how God feeds us exactly what we need (or sometimes takes something away, like your health or maybe your job) to bring us to another level of intimacy with Him. As an example, I will share a quote from a letter my daughter wrote to me before I left for my first surgery.

> …These past days while you have been in pain I have started actually believing in God. Every night I pray that you will get better, and I know that He listens this time. I have never felt this before, but I know He

is there now. I know that God does everything for a
reason and whatever happens is meant to be.

I'm not sure who suffers more, the patient or their spouse
and children. They are the silent victims of this disease, the
ones that fade into the background among the scurry of
activity that surrounds the patient. Without a doubt, there
is more than one fatality when a family receives a cancer
diagnosis. Spouses and children don't get much limelight in
this battle, despite the fact that they are on the front lines
every day. For them there is a fine balance between trying to
keep up a façade of business as usual while trying not to slip
into panic mode. It must be like teetering on the edge of an
abyss.

Moreover, a cancer diagnosis doesn't come with a script,
so we clumsily slip into our roles, making it up as we go along.
There isn't a right or wrong way to deal with this illness,
or death for that matter. The difficulty is determining the
approach that ensures the mental health of the entire family,
which isn't easy, as we all have different coping mechanisms.
For example, mine is 'stillness' while my husband's is the
diametrically opposed 'cleaning the garage.' It takes a lot
of discipline to respect each other's strategy and avoid the
temptation to impose your approach on others. At least we
always know where to find Bob, even though we can't find
anything else that he chooses to "put away" in the garage.

It would be interesting to read the book my family could
write regarding their version of this past year. If I were in
their shoes, I would suspect it would be like walking on
eggshells. You don't want the patient to think you don't
empathize; on the other hand, you still need clean laundry,

rides to school and activities, help with homework, a dress for the dance, maybe a playdate, and even your own TLC. I admit to becoming self-absorbed and, even though I might have had good reason, I also had to remind myself that I was not on this road alone. Not only that, as in most families, there is never just one crisis at a time. My cancer might have been the most urgent problem, but my husband was also unwinding a business, the stock market was in a free fall, and adolescence is no picnic under the best of circumstances.

Most of the responsibilities fell on my husband, which added a burden of guilt to my already heavy heart. I remember after the initial diagnosis, the first thing my sister did was write a prescription for Bob. It made me think of the instructions the stewardess gives before takeoff. "If you're traveling with children, PUT ON YOUR OXYGEN MASK FIRST." Bob needed some well-deserved rest, and if he had to be knocked out to do it, so be it. He was going to be doing a lot of juggling soon and needed to be at peak performance. God doesn't write prescriptions for sedatives, but there are times when I find His words just as soothing.

> *Come to me, all you who are weary and burdened,*
> *and I will give you rest.*
> *Matthew 11:28*

Thank God for my parents who are always ready to step in at a moment's notice, despite their own health challenges. They weren't the only ones either. I am also blessed to live in a town where people have no problem demonstrating what it means to 'love thy neighbor.' There were eager helpers willing to drive, cook, or even change diapers if and when it came to that. Fortunately, I did not have to enlist the diaper changer but have kept her name (*and she knows who she is*) on the list for the future.

Like it or not, we are all in this thing called life 'for better or worse.' All I can say is that it is so much easier when you know you don't have to go through it alone.

> *Yet I am always with you;*
> *You hold me by my right hand.*
> Psalm 73:23

> *Never will I leave you;*
> *never will I forsake you.*
> Hebrews 13:5

> *And surely I am with you always,*
> *to the very end of the age.*
> Matthew 28:20

God helps us rise to any occasion, and He often accomplishes this by using His angels here on earth to sprinkle His mercy and grace where needed. As I said, there was a host of people who offered assistance, and we gratefully accepted support where needed. There may come a time when we will once again need to enlist the army of caring people who volunteered for service, and I have prepared my own *Book of Life* for Bob with their names and numbers, along with their area of expertise, starting with the diaper changer.

Each one should use whatever gift he has received to serve others,
faithfully administering God's grace in its various forms.
1 Peter 4:10

We have different gifts, according to the grace given us.
...If it is serving, let him serve;
...if it is encouraging, let him encourage;
if it is contributing to the needs of others,
let him give generously;
...if it is showing mercy, let him do it cheerfully.
Romans 12:6-8

Scar Issue

There is something beautiful about all scars of whatever nature.
A scar means the hurt is over,
the wound is closed and healed, done with.
                                      Harry Crews

Nobody survives childhood without scars. In fact, when I was growing up, we wore them as a badge of honor. They were evidence of dares taken, adventures shared, and battles fought. As I age, I realize that wrinkles are simply the inevitable scars of time, though few of us wear them with the same bravado. After His resurrection, even Christ had scars. They remain a symbol of His sacrifice on our behalf – a permanent testimony of His undying love for us. In his book, *Everything Belongs*, Richard Rohr notes:

> As they were for Jesus, 'our wounds become honors.'
> The great and merciful surprise is that we come to God
> not by doing it *right* but by doing it *wrong!* [9]

Like so many others, my scars are simply a road map of my life, most of them indicating some mistake or lack of judgment. And those are just the noticeable ones. The ones hidden beneath the surface are the most damaging, but at the same time the least obvious – or maybe not. Psychological and emotional scars, though not physically visible, are the ones that shape your thoughts and contribute most to the person you become. We may not always have control over the experiences that cause those scars, but we always have a choice regarding how we deal with them. We can nurture the healing process and move on, or we can resist it by picking at the scab and reopening the wound repeatedly, allowing it to fester by keeping it exposed too long. It then has the power to infect everything in its path. Therein lies the beauty of God's grace, which allows those wounds to close leaving a beautiful scar as a reminder not of the wound, but of the wisdom we gained through its pain.

Other than the scars from my surgeries, there is no physical evidence of my wrestling match with cancer. And even though the wounds are healed on the surface, the pain is still very much alive where they removed portions of my ribs. Not surprisingly, internal scar tissue takes longer to form and can bring with it a pain of its own. I've learned that sometimes it can become a chronic pain that you just learn to live with.

In my bible study, we were currently reading Genesis, and the story of Jacob's fight with God in chapter 32 resonated strongly with me. Though he held his own, Jacob didn't come away unscathed. You can't experience time with God without being changed. Jacob's scar took the form of a permanent limp, which became an indelible mark of his personal encounter with God.

So Jacob was left alone, and a man wrestled with him till daybreak. When the man saw that he could not overpower him, he touched the socket of Jacob's hip so that his hip was wrenched as he wrestled with the man. Then the man said, "Let me go, for it is daybreak."
But Jacob replied, "I will not let you go unless you bless me."
The man asked him, "What is your name?"
"Jacob," he answered.
Then the man said, "Your name will no longer be Jacob, but Israel, because you have struggled with God and with men and have overcome."
Jacob said, "Please tell me your name."
But he replied, "Why do you ask my name?" Then he blessed him there.
So Jacob called the place Peniel, saying, "It is because I saw God face to face, and yet my life was spared."
The sun rose above him as he passed Peniel, and he was limping because of his hip. Therefore to this day the Israelites do not eat the tendon attached to the socket of the hip, because the socket of Jacob's hip was touched near the tendon.

Genesis 32:24-32

When viewed in this light, the residual pain I was experiencing in my ribs took on new meaning. Rather that being frustrated by it, I needed to embrace it as evidence of what God had brought me through. Maybe that was the point, God didn't want me to "forget about it." Still, this does not mean I'm giving up eating ribs anytime soon.

Recently, while discussing our Catholic elementary school experience, my brother jokingly reminded me, "That which does not kill us makes us stronger." Then again, Nietzsche (whom he was quoting) suffered from chronic health problems and was insane when he died. If I could survive eight years under the nuns' tutelage with my sanity intact, surely I could last at least that long in any cancer arena.

> *Scar tissue is stronger than regular tissue.*
> *Realize the strength, move on.*
> *Henry Rollins*

Easier said than done, but "I can do everything through Him who gives me strength." (Philippians 4:13) Be that as it may, I can't say I've reach Madame Guyon's or St. Augustine's level of enlightenment illustrated in the following quotes, but I have certainly learned to *appreciate* the role of suffering and also to recognize the unique joy and intimacy that can only be found in the midst of it.

> *I have learnt to love the darkness of sorrow;*
> *there you see the brightness of His face.*
> *Madame Guyon*

> *In my deepest wound I see your glory,*
> *and it dazzles me.*
> *St. Augustine*

Matters of Life and Death

There is a certain fear of death
that comes from not having lived yet.
Richard Rohr

During my recuperation from surgery I embraced my love
of theatre with renewed enthusiasm. Not only did I have
a faithful group of attendees, affectionately known as *The
Marvelous Wonderettes,* whose company I cherish, but losing
yourself in a story can be a blissful means of escape – or so
I thought. Unfortunately, every play we saw revolved around
death in some way, shape, or form. For obvious reasons, I
tried to concentrate on comedies only to learn minutes into
each play that the term "comedy" is used loosely in the arts.

Even the best of them had some element of sorrow
woven into the plot with death taking center stage. It dawned
on me rather slowly after months of similar experiences, that
if art imitates life, it is inevitable for pain and sorrow to play
a leading role. They are the crux of true transformation.
Creative genius is often born out of our deepest pain.

It doesn't have to be a literal death. It could be the death
of a relationship, a friend, a family, a job, or in the Christian
vernacular, it is death to 'self' that heralds in a new you,
inevitably changed by events and circumstances usually
beyond our control. At other times, it may be the result of

our own self-destructive behavior. In other words, death is as much a part of life as birth. According to Richard Rohr, once you "exist on a level where we can see how *Everything Belongs*, we can trust the flow and trust the life, the life so large and deep and spacious that it even includes its opposite, death."[10] By accepting life with all its imperfections and what they offer, we learn to accept our own shortcomings and our role in a much larger story. Rohr goes on to say that "those who are totally converted come to every experience and ask not whether or not they liked it, but what does it have to teach them. What's the message in this for me? What's the gift in this for me? How is God in this event? Where is God in this suffering?"[11]

This past weekend I 'suffered' through a show that will remain anonymous. I received a flyer offering discount tickets and advertising two famous comedians as its stars. Thinking this would be a fun way to begin our annual sisters' weekend, I purchased tickets for the three of us who were arriving early. Not being an intellectual, I did not realize the existential nature of this not-so-funny play. Nor was I aware of its Nobel Prize-winning stature or its notoriety. Even the margaritas we consumed at dinner did little to numb our senses to the futility with which the playwright viewed life. We left at intermission conceding that not all suffering is necessary.

I suppose the play might have been the *Seinfeld* of the playwright's era. Both shows are about nothing and everything at the same time. The audience was laughing at times, but the humor was lost on me, and the meaning was beyond my margarita-infused state. Personally, I prefer Seinfeld's version because at least he understood that it's in the nothing where life happens.

The following day I redeemed myself by choosing a classic Broadway extravaganza for the group: lights, music, dancing. But that story, too, had its own share of suffering. To me, it was a truer reflection of life where beauty and suffering are symbiotic. Suddenly, it seemed so obvious. Death is part of everyone's show. Though I've never feared death, I was still trying to evade dwelling on it. I've always considered death as just another step on my journey home – the last step on life's Stairmaster. On the long climb up, I've also learned that, at any point in time, God only gives you "just enough light for the step you're on."[12]

Why was I trying to escape thinking about death? Because I was being barraged with the message to NOT think about it. I discovered a lot of people have trouble admitting their own mortality, or yours for that matter. It's almost as if they believe that by acknowledging it, they will somehow cause it to come sooner. Ironically, the more I tried to tiptoe around the elephant in the room, the more I kept bumping into it. Once I realized it wasn't necessary to avoid reflecting on it, as many suggested, I was free to fall back on my belief that it is not the end, but the beginning of something I'd been in training for my entire life.

I've decided that any show or life that didn't include a liberal dose of pain and sorrow would be boring indeed. Nothing would change. There would be no growth. It would be like ying without yang, light without dark, sun without rain, tears without laughter, happiness without despair, health without illness, life without death. Life would be a vast nothingness that would move as agonizingly slow as the play

I referred to earlier. We live in a world of opposites, which by their coexistence allow the unique beauty of each to be revealed. It is difficult to appreciate one without knowledge of the other.

As William Shakespeare proclaims in *As You Like It*,

> All the world's a stage,
> And all the men and women merely players:
> They have their exits and their entrances;
> And one man in his time plays many parts.

Without question, we all play a role or, as he suggests, many roles in the story of life. There are no auditions or rehearsals. We have no control regarding when we get thrust onto the stage, but we do have control over how we act once we're there. This is where the ability to ad lib can be a valuable asset. The same can be said about our exit. While we have no power over the timing, the style in which it's done is up to us. Life's purest joy is experienced by discovering where we fit into the script and performing our role (or roles) with gusto, trusting God as playwright, producer, and director.

And Dat's De End!

What's Up Doc?
Bugs Bunny

Having cancer is no laughing matter, so you may consider the title a poor choice of words. However, Bugs Bunny's nonchalance epitomizes the God zone I referred to earlier. The place I go to when circumstances are beyond my control or beyond my ability to deal with them. Bugs Bunny's approach to life is not much different. Perhaps he was a Christian. Like me, that silly wabbit was born in Brooklyn, as is evidenced by his heavy New York accent. My husband claims that mine becomes more pronounced after my second glass of wine.

The most striking similarity is our shared tactic in moments of personal peril. His modus operandi is one of "detachment, often quipping, no matter how immediate the danger he was in."[13] Another of his famous phrases was "Of course you realize, this means *war*!" In light of that, I dedicate this chapter to all my prayer warriors who have fought for me so diligently over the past year and continue to do so even as I write.

Initially, the last chapter was to be my eulogy, and began with Porky Pig's famous catchphrase, "That's All Folks," which occasionally was usurped by Bugs Bunny's version,

"And Dat's De End!" However, after my most recent CAT scan, it appears that I will live to see another day. So, while this essay may be the end of this particular episode, only God knows how many more are yet to be written.

When the cancer returned in the fall, I consulted a number of different doctors, including my one and only appointment with Dr. Doom who was callously blunt about his prognosis. You could live anywhere from six weeks to ten years, we just don't know. What he did say was that he did not know of anyone who had been "cured" following a recurrence. That statement didn't leave much to the imagination. The only thing left to determine was where I was going to fall on his mortality scale. Okay, I thought optimistically. Ten years would see my kids through high school and maybe even through college. At least I wouldn't be leaving Bob holding the bag through the tumultuous teenage years. I had two thoughts on Dr. Doom's guesstimate, the first being that on some days death seemed a welcome release from life with two teenagers. The second was, if I had to live through the teenage years, I'd better live long enough for them to be nice to me again. Either way, I seemed to have cheated death for the moment.

The problem with being diagnosed with a terminal illness is that you then mentally prepare yourself for the inevitable, which in my case now may or may not be forthcoming. Life becomes a series of mental calculations focused on just how many times I'd succeed in dodging the bullet. Even if they find something at my next appointment, as long as it is only in one site, I can still address it with surgery, which would give me another year at least. If they find more than one tumor, while chemo won't cure it, it might slow it down and give me more time. Maybe it won't ever come back. Someone has to make up the small percentage of cases where it doesn't reoccur. Why not me? It is enough to drive you crazy. Every event is reduced to a mathematical equation. For example, when I learned my niece was getting married, my first instinct was to calculate the date of the wedding against my own mortality. According to my mental computations, even under a worst-case scenario, I'd still need a dress. I suppose the longer I linger, the less preoccupied I will be with my own demise. I just don't want to become like my father who, despite every doctor's inability to find anything wrong with him, has been predicting his imminent death for the past forty years. He wants "I told you I was sick." engraved on his tombstone. Over the past four months I have planned my funeral (complete with booklet), met with a priest to discuss funeral arrangements, and written my own eulogy and epitaph. What can I say? Genes are a powerful thing.

Prior to my second surgery, the doctors were ultra-conservative with their diagnosis because they did not want to give me false hope, especially because the cancer resurfaced so quickly. They all concurred that with what little they knew about this type of cancer, the probability was high that we had not seen the last of it. In fact, the surgeons didn't even want to operate, they were so convinced it would show up in a second site sooner rather than later. On the other hand, the oncologists didn't suggest chemotherapy or radiation because it is rarely effective on this type of cancer, which would ultimately need to be surgically removed anyway. I was caught in a medical stalemate. In hindsight, surgery appears to have been the right decision and had the added benefit of saving my hair and months of unnecessary treatments.

Following the surgery, there was some discussion of the possibility that the second occurrence stemmed from where the original biopsy was performed. For this reason, the doctors adjusted their prognosis somewhat. The likelihood of it not coming back remains slim, but they seemed to be more optimistic. Not that I'm complaining, but what the heck, or as Bugs Bunny would say, "What's up, Doc?" Three months ago they had me shopping for coffins. Good thing I hadn't started to give away my belongings.

If, in fact, the recurrence was a result of the biopsy, the cancer hadn't spread to a secondary site on its own, which was a good thing. Either way, I was back to square one, starting a new one-year countdown. Not that there are any guarantees that getting through the first year successfully indicates a rare victory, but the odds do improve dramatically. More importantly, the longer it takes to resurface, the more willing they are to operate. With that said, once it moves to multiple sites, they won't chase after it surgically. At that point, I graduate from the surgical team to the oncology team and become a lab rat in clinical trials using drug therapy.

'Plan for the worst, hope for the best' is my strategy. I honestly don't know how people without faith survive the uncertainty of a cancer diagnosis or the endless waiting that comes with it. Life itself becomes your own waiting room. The only reason I have been able to maintain my sanity (or whatever little I possessed to begin with) amidst this health crisis is the fact that I know God is in control and will take care of me and my family.

'For I know the plans I have for you,'
declares the LORD,
' plans to prosper you and not to harm you,
plans to give you hope and a future.'
Jeremiah 29:11

This scripture applies to all of us as God's children. If and when He decides it is my time to leave, He won't take me without providing for those left behind, which was the source of any sadness I felt. That's just not His style.

I've never been very good at following rules, and am famous for pushing the envelope whenever given the opportunity. Yet, relinquishing my problems to God is one of the few commands that I have mastered.

Therefore do not worry about tomorrow,
for tomorrow will worry about itself.
Each day has enough trouble of its own.
Matthew 6:34

Do not be anxious about anything,
but in everything, by prayer and petition, with thanksgiving,
present your requests to God.
And the peace of God, which transcends all understanding,
will guard your hearts and your minds in Christ Jesus.
Phillipians 4:6-7

Who of you by worrying can add a single hour to his life?
Since you cannot do this very little thing,
Why do you worry about the rest?
Luke 22:24

Cast all your anxiety on Him
because He cares for you.
Peter 5:7

Whatever I have (including my life) has been a gift from God, so the least I can do is offer it back.

For whoever wants to save his life will lose it,
but whoever loses his life for me and for the gospel will save it.
Mark 8:35

If people want to follow me,
they must give up the things they want.
They must be willing even to give up their lives to follow me.
Matthew 16:24 (NCV)

There is enormous relief and, odd as it sounds, freedom, in surrendering yourself to God. It doesn't make sense from a human standpoint, but the more you turn over to God the freer you are to become the person for which you were created. C.S. Lewis comments, "The more we let God take us over, the more truly ourselves we become." Your surrender releases you from a self-imposed prison of fear, worry, regret, and control, just to name a few of the feelings that hinder us. God then replaces those life-threatening emotions with His live-giving love, joy, contentment, peace, and purpose.

Peace I leave with you; my peace I give you.
I do not give to you as the world gives.
Do not let your hearts be troubled and do not be afraid.
John 14:27

I have told you these things so that in me you have peace.
In this world you will have trouble.
But take heart. I have overcome the world.
John 16:33

One of Rick Warren's many timely *Purpose Driven Life Daily Devotionals* last week included the following comments which mirror my thoughts and desires so eloquently.

2/17/09
Surrender: Let Go and Let God Work
by Rick Warren

Surrendering your life means:

- Following God's lead without knowing where he's sending you;
- Waiting for God's timing without knowing when it will come;
- Expecting a miracle without knowing how God will provide;
- Trusting God's purpose without understanding the circumstances.

Genuine surrender says, "Father, if this problem, pain, sickness, or circumstance is needed to fulfill your purpose and glory in my life or in another's life, please don't take it away!"

God does speak to you through others, and this was a perfect example.

In closing, knowing what I know about God and Heaven, the kind of fear you might imagine a terminal diagnosis would invoke has never been a variable in any of my endless calculations since the beginning of this crazy ride, nor do I expect it to be in the future. On some level, if I were truly honest, I'd have to admit that any fear I had was not that they *wouldn't* find a cure for my cancer, but that they *would.* I've never viewed death as anything other than returning home into the arms of a welcoming Father. A place where

> *Never again will they hunger;*
> *never again will they thirst.*
> *The sun will not beat upon them,*
> *nor any scorching heat.*
> *For the Lamb at the center of the throne will be their shepherd;*
> *he will lead them to springs of living water.*
> *And God will wipe away every tear from their eyes.*
> *Revelation 7:16-17*

> *He will wipe every tear from their eyes.*
> *There will be no more death or mourning or crying or pain,*
> *for the old order of things has passed away.*
> *He who was seated on the throne said,*
> *'I am making everything new!'*
> *Then he said,*
> *'Write this down, for these words are trustworthy and true.'*
> *Revelation 21:4-5*

In this chaotic world where there is an abundance of joy and beauty, there is also no shortage of pain and suffering. It is a tempting, albeit selfish, thought to be released from our own humanity, to begin an eternal life where there will be no sorrow or pain. If and when I do ultimately succumb to this illness or any other for that matter, I can say without fear, "I know where I came from and where I am going." (John 8:14b) And for that reason alone I can cease my mental computations. I don't need to know what's going to happen in the future, nor do I need to fear tomorrow, or the one after that, or the one after that, and so on. Why worry how many days I might have left, when I've got this one now just waiting to be lived? If death is the absence of living, then I could either be counted among the walking dead by obsessing about tomorrow, or I could abandon my worries and live in the moment. God asks only that I stop thinking about the dying and concentrate on the living, taking it one day at a time. I think I can manage that – at least today I can "because He lives."

Because He Lives
Music and Lyrics by William J. Gaither © 1971

Because He lives, I can face tomorrow.
Because He lives, all fear is gone.
Because I know He holds the future,
And life is worth the living
just because He lives.

Tribble Triplets

There is hope, for me yet, because God won't forget,
all the plans he's made for me
I have to wait and see,
He's not finished with me yet, He's not finished with me yet.
Wait and See
Brandon Heath, 2008

By now it is safe to say that you know the important parts of my story; but most people have never heard of me, and I'm not surprised. There is nothing that memorable or out of the ordinary about me, which is an important piece of what I am about to say. I could have been anyone until December 18th, 2007, when I was diagnosed with this rare form of cancer called a retroperitoneal liposarcoma. Up until that point I never thought about my death—it seemed so far away, and still might be for all I know. What I came to appreciate after that day was that we all live in a world full of uncertainty...a world where you can be hit with a cancer diagnosis, a world where you can lose a loved one, a world where an errant driver can cause a deadly collision, a world where terrorism can strike, a world where your finances and security can be decimated in a day. Our lives can *and do* change in an instant.

There is nothing unique about me. We all struggle in our lives. It is the nature of the beast. You don't have to be diagnosed with cancer to feel the pain of being human. Whether it is physical or emotional, hurting seems to be an unavoidable element of the human condition. To be honest, I'm not sure cancer is the foremost disease for which I need a cure. There are other pressing ones that have caused more pain in my life than cancer. The hurts, hang-ups, and habits that most of us struggle with aren't rare at all. Life is a smorgasbord of blessings and problems too. My guess is that a majority of people feel their plate is heavily weighted on the problem side. Sometimes we choose our own poison, other times it is thrust upon us. Whether it is cancer, pride, selfishness, bitterness, fear, guilt, anxiety, anger, loneliness, infidelity, or addiction, we all need to understand how to grasp God's healing power.

It is His power that allows me to live everyday in peace knowing that my time may be limited. It is His power that prevented me from falling apart in September 2008 when my second cancer was discovered. It is His power that allowed me to remain so pragmatic when my third cancer surfaced six months later. And His power is available to everyone. It comes through His gift of faith. There is a website you might be familiar with called *FaithMattersNow*, and I couldn't agree more because, let's face it, life is messy.

I wouldn't recommend waiting until you're in the midst of a crisis to accept and open God's gift of faith by developing a relationship with Christ, though more often than not, that's exactly when He becomes real for many of us. As Rick Warren suggests, "Our lives change more through the crisis we experience than through the creed we confess."[14] I studied the Bible for many years before what I was learning in my head finally reached my heart. It wasn't until I found myself totally reliant on God that all my knowledge came alive and was transformed into a deep personal faith. And strangely, it wasn't *my* cancer; it was someone else's that forged my newfound intimacy with Christ.

The message I hope to convey through *I Don't Buy Green Bananas* is the importance of faith. Not my faith, God's faith. Faith is a gift from God, so my faith is going to look a lot different from yours, which is exactly why it is important for all of us to share our stories. They combine to create a bigger picture of God. Ephesians 2:8 says

> *For it is by grace you have been saved, through faith –*
> **and this not from yourselves, it is the gift of God –**
> *not by works, so that no one can boast.*

We are all unique, so God in His wisdom tailors His gift to suit each and every one of us. It has been said that God meets us where we are, so it's no wonder that each of our relationships with him will be different, even as our own will be day to day. Faith is not static; it ebbs and flows, grows and matures, and sometimes seems elusive. However, God never takes back a gift, so you can be sure if you are having difficulty being faithful, it is you.....not Him. As my friend always says, if you feel distant from God, it's you that's moved, not Him. And because faith is His gift, He's the one who will help you rediscover it in your weakest moments. Those are the times when we need to draw near to him, so that He can carry us to the other side of our pain.

Let me begin by giving you my most recent example of how God works in my life. Over the past several months I have been praying for guidance, asking God what He wanted me to do next. For months I heard, "Hold in stillness." For those of you who have experienced cancer, being in a holding pattern is quite common. And it's not necessarily a bad place to be. I had no trouble being still this summer and had a lovely tan to prove it. However, come September I was starting to get restless as if there was something I was supposed to be doing but didn't know what it was. Again, I prayed for guidance. God's answer didn't seem logical, but it rarely does. He wanted me to write a speech. It was straight out of *Field of Dreams.* "If you build it, they will come." I learned a long time ago that "Mine is not to reason why, mine is but to do or die." I never knew where this quote originated, but recently learned it is from Tennyson's *Charge of the Light Brigade,* which is hilarious because that is just the way I approach life. *Charge!* I know I'm not alone in this approach. I see armies of people everyday charging out of Starbucks, armed with liquid energy, onto life's battleground.

The thing is, any time you stop to question why and choose not to obey God, you take another step further away from him, and your relationship wilts a little. Take enough of these baby steps, and you will eventually find yourself quite distant from the place you need to be – at the feet of Jesus.

Even knowing all this, my first reaction was, "Oh come on. I don't have anything to say that people would want to hear." His answer made me laugh out loud. "No kidding, but I do. Now sit down and write." So, I wrote the speech. Had no idea where it was going to be delivered, just put it in my bag and waited. You never know when someone is going to ask you to give a speech. I wanted to be prepared.

I have to confess, that's not entirely true. As usual, I couldn't resist putting my own two cents in. I thought maybe it was for my Bible Study women so I sent a copy off to the Teaching Director. Shame on me. You'd think I'd know by now that God had a bigger statement to make. The week after I finished it, I walked into Bible Study and someone handed me a note asking if I would be willing to speak at her church. I couldn't help but chuckle. God is so good to me despite my feeble attempts to offer my input. Naturally, He had His audience chosen. I told her not only would I be willing, but it was already written. It would have been a good story if I went on to deliver the speech, but what happened next makes it an even better one.

When I contacted the church about the invitation, the coordinator invited me to stop by and meet her to discuss details. On fire with what I thought was a mission from God, I *"charged"* in to introduce myself. When I shared my Godwink about how the speech came about, I expected her to be in awe of God's handiwork. "That's nice," she replied, "but we don't really want you to give a speech." A brief sample from the book and a short question and answer session was what they had in mind. "What? Doesn't she realize I am on a mission from God?" Feeling a little foolish and more than a bit deflated, I responded, "Great. I'd be happy to oblige." Still, I knew there was someone God intended it for besides me, and I was sure He would let me know where and to whom it was to be delivered.

His audience of one was revealed to me weeks later. You might think it a stretch to think that God would go to all that trouble to reach one soul. I can't emphasize enough that He is a personal God, which means that's EXACTLY what He does. This doesn't change the fact that others (including myself) may now be encouraged by that same speech. The unique beauty of God's language of love is that it always feels as if He is speaking directly to you.

What became obvious through this process was that it was never meant to be a speech, but another chapter. It took on a life of its own, affecting everyone in its wake. As I witnessed the influence it had on the first few individuals to whom it was delivered, I realized the topics of hurting, healing, and hope are universal. Not only that, it became the sample I shared from *I Don't Buy Green Bananas,* which was probably His intention all along. Public speaking is not one of the gifts God has blessed me with. He just wanted me to read the words He provided. Listening to God is not an exact science and involves a lot of trial and error. Thankfully, if you don't get it right the first time, God maneuvers things in such a way that you are guided along, even if you don't recognize His efforts on your behalf (which are easier to see in hindsight for most people.) Serving God doesn't require perfect hearing, but it does require a willingness to yield to His plans and not our own.

Now, about this book. The only criticisms I've heard about it is that there is too much God and Bible stuff in it. If you skipped over that, I was told, it isn't half bad. My thought is, if you skipped over that, not only did you miss the point, but it is no longer a book but a pamphlet. It never ceases to amaze me the garbage people will tolerate from the media, but once you bring God into the equation, that's when people start to balk. It's okay to write about sex and violence as long as you don't discuss God; though, believe me, there is plenty of sex and violence in the Bible. Personally, I believe there is a silent majority out there that enjoys hearing about how God works in the lives of others. And I also believe that we shouldn't be embarrassed to discuss it. How sad that people would be offended by that kind of message but be totally comfortable with the glut of Cialis and Viagra ads we are bombarded with daily.

Whether you like the book or not, people who read it or view my video may think the journey I'm on is not a difficult one. Just because I choose not to dwell on the pain of the experience doesn't make it any less real. Oddly, many people would prefer to hear the gory details than about the lessons I learned through them. Sometimes, I think they are surprised to find me looking normal – not green and bald from chemo treatments. The upside to my type of cancer is that I don't have to suffer through those treatments because it doesn't respond to any known drug therapies. The flipside is that there is no treatment other than surgery, which eventually will no longer be an option either. Yes, I've discovered a new level of pain I hope never to revisit and suffered the indignities most patients do in the hospital. However, it is always a choice as to what you carry away with you after any experience.

One of the things I discovered about myself through this experience is something that many of us share – a propensity for "filling in the blanks." John Eldridge describes this habit in his book, *Walking With God.* He writes,

> We are constantly filling in the blanks of what we think God is up to instead of asking him. (*And here's the important part*) **It isn't helpful**. It's taking the ball and running with it, leaving God behind.[15]

He goes on to remind us of God's words in Isaiah 55:8

"For my thoughts are not your thoughts,
neither are your ways my ways," declares the LORD.

God knows what's ahead. He knows what I need. I can either trust Him or not. It was an enormous freedom to release my need to know what's coming and my natural inclination to "fill in the blanks." The most helpful thing I could do was to "be still and know that He is God." (Psalm 46:10) In doing so, I leave my worries at His feet so that I can enjoy whatever He has in store for me *today*. It's not that I don't *think* about the cancer. I just don't *worry* about it. Believe me, there isn't a minute of any day when it is far from my mind. It just isn't with a sense of fear or foreboding. It is more like, "I wonder where He's going with this or what He wants me to do with it" – confident that He will reveal the next step only when He thinks I am ready. I just need to be patient and peaceful, to stay close and quiet enough to hear Him. Too many of us fill in the blanks with busyness, charging forward until there is so much noise in our lives we miss God's lesson and purpose for us.

With all that said, I have to admit there are unexpected moments when I see something that triggers a reflex that I have to make a conscious effort to stop. For example, seeing a grandmother holding her grandchild and suddenly feeling that my heart might shatter with the thought of never seeing my grandchildren. Or attending a wedding and being overwhelmed with sadness wondering if I will get to see my daughter walk down the aisle or my son standing at the altar eagerly awaiting his bride. When those moments happen, I think of Paul's words in 2 Corinthians 10, "we take captive every thought to make it obedient to Christ." Yes, I have to deliberately capture the thought and give it to God with the understanding that if that is His plan, it's because He's got something even better in mind.

Do you remember the saying, "The mind is the devil's workshop?" That's because our thoughts determine our actions. Nothing offends Satan more than seeing a Christian joyful amidst suffering. No, he wants to see us in the depths of despair. Why? Because misery loves company, and you can't minister to others if you are drowning in despair.

Everyone has to develop their own devices to stem these kind of negative thoughts. My friend use to look over her shoulder, say, "Thanks for sharing," then flick it away. I like to remember Jesus casting out demons from people in the gospels and remind myself that we can tap into that same power. Peter instructs us to **"Cast all our** anxiety on Jesus."(1 Peter 5:7) and Mark 16:17 assures us that we will be given the power to do so. "And these signs will accompany those who believe: In my name they will drive out demons."

That's why I enjoy studying the Bible – to remind myself of God's power, promises, and sovereignty. Here is an entire book spanning over 500 years revealing God's character. And it is not "until we understand God's true character that we can completely trust Him."[16] The author of the book, *Be Joyful*, explains it much better than I ever could. He states,

> You see, when we trust that God is in control of all things – the good, the bad, and the ugly – we can be joyful because we know that God is working behind the scenes for our good and His glory.[17]

Recently, a friend and I were discussing our experiences facing cancer. We both agreed that the very thing that hurt us by worldly standards was also the thing that healed us on a much deeper level. It was through the pain that we learned to trust God and to experience the inner peace and joy that only God can provide. I've heard some people refer to facing difficult times as "testing." I think a more accurate phrase would be teaching. Remember the story of Abraham and Isaac? I've been taught all my life that God was testing Abraham's faith, but I never accepted that explanation. I don't think God tests; I believe he teaches. What was He teaching Abraham and Isaac? A lesson Abraham would never forget, which is illustrated by the name he chose for that place as a reminder for generations to come of the valuable lesson he learned that day.

> *Abraham called that place The LORD Will Provide.*
> *And to this day it is said,*
> *"On the mountain of the LORD it will be provided."*
> *Genesis 22:14*

At some point in our lives, we will all find ourselves on the mountaintop, at which time we will either have to take a leap of faith or fall off the cliff. My belief is that God will never ask us to climb that mountain without providing the courage, the strength, or the means to accomplish the task. All He asks from us is trust.

I don't know if any of you have read about the new saints that were recently canonized. One of them is a Fr. Damien. The second documented miracle he performed was to cure a woman of the same type of cancer as mine, which is pretty rare. There are only two in 1,000,000 cases reported annually.

In 1997 after Audrey Toguchi's cancer spread to her lungs and she was given six months to live, she visited Fr. Damien's gravesite with her two sisters and asked the priest, "Please, please pray for me." A month later, her doctor noticed the cancer was shrinking. In four months it was gone. Astonished, the doctor asked what she had done. She told him, "You just gotta trust. You gotta have faith."[18]

After hearing the story, my daughter immediately said, "Go see him!" I told her that, besides the fact that he's been dead for over a century, I believe his grave is in Hawaii. "So go to Hawaii." If God wants to heal me, I replied, he knows where I am, I don't need to fly to Hawaii. I didn't express my belief that just because a miracle may have been the purpose of Audrey Toguchi's cancer, that doesn't mean it's the purpose of mine. Then again, isn't being able to face cancer with joy a miracle in itself? Frankly, I think God makes a bigger statement by NOT healing me. Who wouldn't be joyful having been cured of a life-threatening illness? The real challenge is having faith and joy in the absence of a miracle. Even the guard who arrested Jesus must have experienced a new-found faith after Jesus reattached his ear. Most people probably wouldn't even attribute the remission to God. However, it is hard to dismiss someone who is joyful despite his circumstances.

Maybe the purpose of my cancer is to illustrate joy without the cure. Suffering people are more inclined to listen to someone in the same boat. Let's face it; miracles are not the norm. Even when Jesus lived, He didn't choose to heal everyone. I don't doubt for a second that miracles exist and happen everyday, but we can't expect to understand the how, why, or when God uses them, nor should we. Isn't that how we ended up here? Adam and Eve's desire to know everything God knew. Well, you can't know the good without the bad, so I think they got more than they bargained for.

Most of us are faced with reality which, unfortunately, doesn't always include a miraculous solution to our suffering. To be honest, I'm not even sure I'd want a miracle. My illness has brought me closer to God than I ever thought possible. My fear is that if I am cured, I would eventually become complacent again. Then I am reminded of something I was taught about how a shepherd trains a lamb that has a tendency to stray. He breaks its legs, then carries it around on his shoulders until they heal. By the time the lamb is able to walk on his own again, it is so attached to the shepherd that it never leaves his side. My joy doesn't depend on a miracle; it depends on my relationship with Christ, my ability to stay close to Him regardless of my circumstances, and my ability to trust in His promises.

Last October, after the doctor reluctantly agreed to perform a second surgery, his nurse was running through final instructions with me for the day of the operation. As my husband and I listened, the surgeon (who seemed to be having second thoughts) stuck his head in the room to mention this caveat. "You know you're going to be back here six months from now, right?" My immediate thought was, "Maybe, but that's six more months than if I don't have the surgery." Although his lack of confidence was clear, no one offered any other viable option except doing nothing, which didn't look too promising either. Not only that, the fact that he was so sure I'd still be around in six months was the best news I'd heard thus far.

Well, he must be an even better doctor than I thought because, almost six months to the day, I did indeed find myself back in his office presenting a new lump to add to my growing list of tribbles. Oddly enough, I made the discovery the very same day I sent my *Green Bananas* manuscript to the publisher. Hoping this was the final act of my *Tribble Trilogy*, I sat patiently waiting to see the doctor. Fortunately, he was able to extract this one without a major surgery. It was very *Young Frankensteinish*. He performed the tribblectomy in his office using a local anesthetic, chatting away while digging for treasure. I kept telling him to stop talking and concentrate on what he was doing, but he seemed totally comfortable doing both. In what seemed like a Gene Wilder moment, he boasted, "Got it!" as he held up the newest addition to my "triblets."

I'm not sure yet whether God wants me to pen a sequel to my *Green Bananas* book. If I am on the six-month installment plan, maybe he intends to keep me around and just take me one piece at a time. All I know is that there must be some reason I am still here while my Aunt Anne, who was diagnosed shortly before me, is not; nor any of the other thousands of cancer patients who do not survive. While I am not a pessimist, I am a realist. I am painfully aware that the odds are not in my favor. However, any day I wake up is considered a good day – a perfect day to celebrate the gift of life and the opportunity to share it's joys and sorrows with others. I want to pay homage to those who have gone before me by using whatever reprieve God's given me in a way that honors their memory and God's decision to spare me for the moment. As the song says, "He's up to something." I haven't figured out what it is, but I am convinced there is something He still wants me to do. No, He's not finished me with yet, or else I wouldn't be sitting here writing.

One last thing, just because I don't dwell on my health problems doesn't mean I don't get moody, depressed, or irritable. I am still the same menopausal maniac I was before the cancer diagnosis. I am not one of those annoying Life is Good advocates because, while God is good, life isn't always. I still have good days and bad days, as my family will attest. They just aren't driven by fear or anxiety about cancer. No, the cause is usually much more mundane – things like spending hours in the car driving the kids around, chores I'd rather not do, the month of rain we experienced this summer, or being told to "chill" by my daughter. Little does she know, this is me *AFTER* the so-called chill pill. Honestly, the only fear I have is reaching the end of my life without discovering or accomplishing God's purpose for me.

Having faith doesn't make you a perfect person or guarantee a perfect life. It helps you accept that you're not and never will be, and neither is life. Not only that, it offers comfort in the knowledge that God loves you anyway and will be with you always to help you along your journey through a broken world and bring you home to Him - where we will finally learn the meaning of perfection. Faith allows you to experience God's love, and believe me, it is irresistible to be loved liked that. It is a love that has the ability to make each of us feel like His favorite. When you truly understand the depth of His love, all else fades away. It transforms the way you view the world, your circumstances, and your role in them. The beauty of being a Christian is that our foundation is in Christ so that when our world begins to crumble around us, we can remain strong in the shelter of our Father's love. This doesn't mean we don't hurt, break, or suffer. It means we can persevere under the harshest of circumstances knowing that

"God works for the good of those who love him, who have been called according to his purpose." (Romans 8:27-29)

I wish I could leave you with a simple formula to discover your own faith. There isn't one. It's a process. God has a plan for each of us and will reveal Himself to everyone in different ways at different times. However, I can tell you that searching and asking is always an excellent place to start. Like all relationships, the ones we cherish and work on are the ones that last. Your relationship with God is one you can't afford to ignore. If nothing else, practice "being still," and listen to what He has to say. I think our biggest obstacle is busyness. We have no problem asking, but we take off, charging through our day without listening for His answer. Here's the trick. Let God lead the charge, and be amazed at where He leads you.

My son and I watched a movie recently called *Forever Strong*. It is based on the true story of Larry Gelwix, a rugby coach in Salt Lake City. The message this man taught his team was simply "learn to listen," not to him but to the inner voice that guides you to become the man you were created to be. Who does he attribute this voice to? God. The coach's stated goal was to make the young men forever strong on the field so they could be forever strong in life. His idea of winning was not based on the scoreboard. Even though life is the only playing field most of us will ever walk on, learning to listen takes training, discipline and hard work, but as Paul says in 1 Corinthians 9:25:

> *Everyone who competes in the games goes into strict training.*
> *They do it to get a crown that will not last;*
> *but we do it to get a crown that will last forever.*

Athletes train for a season; we train for eternity. Effective training doesn't happen in a day. It takes time and perseverance. John Baker comments in his book, *Life's Healing Choices:*

> We live in a world of instant everything: mashed potatoes, coffee, microwave popcorn, even information. And we want instant spiritual maturity. One day we are a total mess, and we want to be Billy Graham the next. It doesn't happen that way. There's an old saying, "Life by the yard is hard, but by the inch, it's a cinch." You grow by inches. You experience victory day by day. Jesus tells us, "Don't be anxious about tomorrow. God will take care of your tomorrow too. Live one day at a time."[19]

Did you know there are over 7,000 promises from God in the Bible? Pick out a few and memorize them as a constant reminder of His love for you. You don't need to be a Bible scholar to find them. In the NIV Bible, you can look in the index and pick the areas in which you struggle. It will direct you to relevant verses. Or you can use Google or Biblegateway.com. Do yourself a favor. Pick short ones; they are easier to remember. Here are a few quick examples.

Having trouble sleeping?

> *Come to me, all you who are weary and burdened,*
> *and I will give you rest.*
> *Matthew 11:28*

Are you a worrier?

Therefore do not worry about tomorrow,
for tomorrow will worry about itself.
Each day has enough trouble of its own.
Matthew 6:34

Are you anxious?

Cast all your anxiety on him because he cares for you.
1 Peter 5:7

Feeling fearful?

Do not be afraid, for I am with you.
Genesis 26:24

Lonely?

And surely I am with you always, to the very end of age.
Matthew 28:20

Need strength/courage?
This is the one Tim Tebow, the Heisman-award winning quarterback, wears on his face in every game.

I can do everything through him who gives me strength.
Phillipians 4:13

If I ever lose my hair from experimental treatments, I am going to tattoo this one on my head. Until then, I will close with one of my favorites that I rely on daily, and it comes from Jeremiah 29:11.

"For I know the plans I have for you," declares the Lord,
"plans to prosper you and not to harm you,
plans to give you hope and a future."

I don't know what the future holds any more than you do. My hope and joy doesn't depend on a future here, but a future with God regardless of where I am. It's in His promises that I trust.

Let Go and Let God

So then, let us not be like others, who are asleep,
but let us be alert and self-controlled.
1 Thessalonians 5:6

You'd think at this point I would have mastered letting go and letting God do His thing, in His time. But no-o-o-o-o! Even after two years of divine coddling, I found myself doing exactly what I discussed in the previous chapter – sitting in the waiting room at Sloane Kettering *"filling in the blanks."* During the weeks leading up to my six-month checkup, I had mentally prepared myself for the worst, especially since I had not been feeling well for some time. When the doctor gave me a thumbs-up, I was shocked. You are going to think this is crazy, but my good news caused an unexpected faith crisis.

In presuming I understood God's plan and timing, I had become convinced of my own destiny, which in my mind was death. What had I missed along the way? What was I supposed to be doing while I was so self-absorbed with writing my own exit scene? How could I have gotten it so wrong? And if I got this wrong, how many other things did I misinterpret? I felt like a fool and a failure.

What joys had I missed in my haste to sprint ahead? It was a humbling experience to realize how susceptible I am, and how subtle Satan can be in undermining your relationship with Christ. The audience of one I spoke of in the previous chapter was me. It was no coincidence that God had me writing again a month before my appointment. He was trying to keep me alert so that I wouldn't become a victim of my own arrogance. Christianity is a life-long process, and any time you feel like you've finally got it, you are setting yourself up for a fall.

My daughter, who knows me better than I think, wasn't far off when she told my friend, "My mom's disappointed she's not going to die." It was difficult to explain to her that my disappointment was not due to the test results but my own recidivism. How quickly and easily I slipped back into my old ways. By having me write the previous chapter, God was reminding me once again to let go and let Him handle my life *and death*. Even my Bible study lesson the week before gave me a timely reminder, which unfortunately went unheeded.

> We get into trouble when we don't let the Lord determine our agenda. Rarely does God call us and provide a five-year plan. Most of the time He calls us to take one step and then another, teaching us to trust and obey as we go.

My brutally honest girlfriend summed up the experience beautifully by pointing out that, "You're disappointed because you realized you're only human – just like the rest of us." I thought back to the 'why me' and 'why not me' question. What made me think I wouldn't be just as vulnerable as anyone else to letting my thoughts run wild? Even the lesson I completed in the waiting room warned, "We are never closer to defeat than in our moments of greatest victory." It then goes on to say,

> Often discouragement sets in after great spiritual experiences, especially those requiring physical effort or involving great emotion...Elijah's battles were not over; there was still work for him to do. When you feel let down after a great spiritual experience, remember that God's purpose for your life is not yet over.[20]

I'm no Elijah, but you don't need to be a prophet for God to use you. He has a purpose for all of us. He still had work for me to do and proved it by giving me another opportunity the following week to minister to others. I was reminded once again that you don't need a huge audience to affect people's lives. Dramatic exhibitions are not the way God works these days. He taught me something in composing the last chapter so that I, in turn, could share it with others. It wasn't His plan that He revealed; it was His love. And there is no greater privilege than to be able to share that love with those around you.

I believe He was also speaking in a gentle whisper to a new friend who turned out to be His next audience of one. Do you know what I think He was saying? A simple "Hello," which brings up another point made in last week's Bible Study lesson that "God's power to quietly move an individual soul demonstrates His great might." Those kind of heavenly interventions happen everyday.

The night after my visit to New York, my daughter saw me engrossed in something and asked what I was reading, which happened to be my own book. Wise beyond her years, and in a way that only she can, she queried, "Trying to figure out where you went wrong?" I was indeed trying to determine how I had gotten so far off course from where I was when I wrote the previous chapter just a month ago. How could I be telling people not to do exactly what I had just done? It was a lesson in humility, and one God wanted me to illustrate. Despite the intimacy I felt with God during the two years since my diagnosis, I still managed to find myself in the dangerous position of trying to determine my own fate. Somehow, I had temporarily forgotten all that I learned through my experience. The *divine dissatisfaction* I felt with my spiritual condition at that moment could have been discouraging if I didn't use it to strengthen my faith. Warren Wiersbe comments in his book, *Be Joyful*, that "divine dissatisfaction is essential for spiritual growth."[21] I needed to recognize my limitations and build up my spiritual arsenal in preparation for the next time I am in the same situation. I chose the following scripture to memorize for obvious reasons. I needed to stop beating myself up and recognize that my weakness is exactly what keeps me close to God. By embracing it, I allow myself to submit; which, in turn, opens my heart to be filled with His strength.

> *Three times I pleaded with the Lord to take it away from me. But he said to me 'My grace is sufficient for you, for my power is made perfect in weakness.' Therefore I will boast all the more gladly about my weaknesses, so that Christ's power may rest on me. That is why, for Christ's sake, I delight in weaknesses, in insults, in hardships, in persecutions, in difficulties. For when I am weak, then I am strong.*
>
> *2 Corinthians 12:8-10*

"Blessed are the meek," says Jesus in the Sermon on the Mount (Matthew 5:5). It took me a long time to understand that verse. In a society that prides itself on personal achievement, it seems counter intuitive. However, the meek realize their need for God's power and don't rely on themselves, which actually puts them in a position of great strength. God gave us all unique abilities that He expects us to use. We can't "Let go and let God" to the point of being incapacitated, but in the end we will only get so far on our own. When we start to value our gifts more than the giver, we are in dangerous territory. Our real strength lies in our ability to recognize our own weakness and His authority. I read stories everyday about people who "beat" cancer, attributing their victory to anything from positive attitude to an organic diet. A positive attitude certainly helps, as will a healthy diet and many other practices that are within our control. However, ultimately, the decision is God's alone, and no one can claim control over that, or predict it, for that matter. His timing is even less obvious.

My spiritual faux pas is a glaring warning that it takes diligence and discipline to avoid becoming complacent in your spiritual life. We are all a work-in-progress until we die, and the moment you forget that, your spirituality begins to deteriorate; and you are ripe for temptation. Even with all that said, let me add in my defense that I was the one who found the last two lumps and have been told to "listen to my body." I just mistook "I'm old and achy" for "The cancer is back." I guess my hearing is going as well.

Don't misunderstand. I wasn't disappointed to learn that my symptoms were a result of aging, which, unfortunately, they haven't discovered a cure for either. My disappointment stemmed from finding myself so far from where I needed to be – following Christ, not racing ahead. I was reminded of walking with my children as youngsters. I'd let them run ahead, but when I thought they were getting too far away or approaching danger, I'd yell, "STOP!" My visit to Sloane was God's "STOP!" which I heard loud and clear.

Like it or not, I find myself back at square one, exactly where I started this book – a classic example of human weakness and a walking reminder to

clothe yourselves with humility toward one another, because, 'God opposes the proud but gives grace to the humble.' Humble yourselves, therefore, under God's mighty hand, that he may lift you up in due time. Cast all your anxiety on him because he cares for you.

Be self-controlled and alert. Your enemy the devil prowls around like a roaring lion looking for someone to devour. Resist him, standing firm in the faith, because you know that your brothers throughout the world are undergoing the same kind of sufferings.

And the God of all grace, who called you to his eternal glory in Christ, after you have suffered a little while, will himself restore you and make you strong, firm and steadfast. To him be the power for ever and ever. Amen.

1 Peter 5:5-11

Blood Relatives

You don't choose your family.
They are God's gift to you, as you are to them.
Desmond Tutu

Being the fourth in a family of seven, I know a little about growing up in someone's shadow. My older siblings were a hard act to follow in school, and there were frequent doubts as to whether or not we shared the same parents. Yet, despite my often rebellious attitude, I actually enjoyed being in my family's shadow, except when I was waiting in line for the bathroom. I was proud to be known as so-and-so's daughter or little sister, or big sister. My family was my security. I knew where I belonged and so did everyone else in the neighborhood. Of course, that meant that I rarely got away with anything because there was nowhere to hide. Though Brooklyn is a far cry from the South, a southern friend of mine recalls her own mom's warning, "If they don't know you, they'll know your mother!" (or father, or brother, or sister.)

As a little sister, I was either a failure or an enormous success if you measured it by how miserable I could make life for my older siblings. Whatever I lacked intellectually, my older sister (and younger ones for that matter) more than made up for. Not one to fade into the background gracefully, I took full advantage of my elder sister's brains (and not the ones she kept in the fridge for her science experiments). I still feel guilty for the time I stole one of her poems, entered it into a contest, and WON! Ironic that I would be the one to end up writing. I also inherited her Girl Scout sash full of badges and proudly paraded around as if I had earned them all.

In an attempt to redeem myself for the poem theft and the Girl Scout charade, all proceeds of *I Don't Buy Green Bananas* are being donated to her current science project. My sister, Mary Frances Horowitz, MD, MS, is now the Chief Scientific Director of the Center for International Blood & Marrow Transplant Research (CIBMTR) at the Medical College of Wisconsin. In elementary school she followed the brain project with a blood one, replacing the brains in the fridge with vials of her blood specimens. They served as a good appetite suppressant (which I needed badly at the time) every time I went in search of a snack.

I don't know if those grade school projects were the beginning of her career in medicine, but her many awards and accolades come as no surprise to me. She may be my big sister, but through her work at CIBMTR she can assume that role for so many others by helping them determine the proper course of treatment, as she did for me.

The Center for International Blood and Marrow Transplant Research is an organization made up of clinical and basic research scientists from around the world who share data on their blood and bone marrow transplant patients to improve the success of these procedures for all. It is *not a donor registry*, but a confidential repository of information about *results* of transplants from more than 450 transplant centers worldwide.

Across the globe, diversity is celebrated. People vary in many exciting ways, including age and racial origin. These same differences, however, can make the science of treating cancer and other life-threatening diseases difficult. Diversity means that the best treatment for one patient might not be the same as the best treatment for another, even if they have the same disease. It is often difficult for individual treatment centers to examine these differences and draw conclusions as to what treatments may be most successful for each of their patients. Only by sharing experiences among many research centers can such questions be answered.

CIBMTR's mission is to improve the outcomes of blood and bone marrow transplantation, a complex therapy used to treat cancers of the blood and immune system and other life-threatening diseases. They accomplish this by gathering data on many transplant results and analyzing the information to see what treatments are the most effective for which patients. They then share this information with the worldwide community of patients, physicians and other researchers. To date, they have disseminated this information in more than 400 articles in textbooks and medical journals.

The National Institutes of Health and the Health Resources and Services Administration provides 75 percent of the funding for CIBMTR activities. The remainder comes from corporations, foundations and individuals. These contributions are essential for the CIBMTR to continue its life-saving work.

To learn more about CIBMTR, please visit their website, www.cibmtr.org.

If you feel so inclined, donations can be sent to:

Sherry L. Fisher
CIBMTR
Medical College of Wisconsin
9200 W. Wisconsin Avenue
CLCC, Suite C5500
Milwaukee, WI 53226

CIBMTR, Center for International Blood & Marrow Transplant Research is a 501(c)(3) non-profit organization. Contributions are tax deductible as allowed by law.

Post-Script from a Proud Older Sister

I am honored to have Joan end this book with a description of my science projects - and the work I have been involved with for the past 25 years. It is work that I am proud of as it focuses on finding effective treatments for people with many different kinds of serious illnesses, including several types of cancer.

However, I am even more proud to have Joan as a sister - her energy, intelligence, incredible organizational skills, sense of humor, fierce devotion to family and friends and concern for those in need have been gracing our family's lives - and the lives of many others - for years. She won't tell you this, but while I may have gotten the science fair awards, Joanie was always the person that people liked to have around. Anyone who has read her books will not wonder why. It has been an honor to share Joan's current journey through cancer with her in some small way - her honesty, common sense, love and faith give "joy" to all around her.

Mary Maresca Horowitz

P.S. I never knew (or maybe my 55-year-old brain has forgotten) about the poem or the Girl Scout badges - but glad they were of use.

183

"*Finally, all we have to give away is our own journey. Our own story. Then we become living witnesses. The only authority we have in other people's lives is what we ourselves have walked and what we know to be true. Then we have earned the right to speak...We must believe in such a way that we give hope and meaning to the next generation...That's what our lives are for: to hand on the mystery to those who are coming after us, which means that we have to appropriate the mystery ourselves.*"

Richard Rohr
Everything Belongs

Endnotes

Unless otherwise noted, all scripture references were taken from the HOLY BIBLE, NEW INTERNATIONAL VERSION, Copyright 1973, 1978, 1984 by International Bible Society. Used by permission of Zondervan Publishing House. All rights reserved.

[1] HOLY BIBLE, NEW INTERNATIONAL VERSION, Copyright 1973, 1978, 1984 by International Bible Society, 1204.

[2] Walker, John, *The Purpose Driven Life Daily Devotional, Do Your Best to Rest*, PurposeDrivenLife.com, September 2, 2008.

[3] Wikipedia, *Star Trek: The Trouble with Tribbles*, ttp:// en.wikipedia.org/wiki/The_Trouble_with_Tribbles

[4] Wikipedia, *The Last Holiday*, en.wikipedia.org/wiki/Last_ Holiday_(2006_film).

[5] Young, William P., *The Shack*, (Newbury Park, California, Windblown Media, 2007) 182.

6   Feiler, Bruce, *Abraham, A Journey to the Heart of Three Faiths*, (New York, New York, HarperCollins Publishers, 2002, 2004) 6.

7   Lewis, C.S., *The Chronicles of Narnia: Price Caspian*, (Walden Media, Walt Disney) 2008.

8   Tada, Joni Eareckson, *A Step Further*, (Grand Rapids, Michigan, Zondervan, 1978, 1990, 2001) 88.

9   Rohr, Richard, *Everything Belongs*, (New York, New York, The Crossroad Publishing Company, 1999, 2003) 21.

10   Ibid, 33.

11   Ibid, 91.

12   Omartian, Stormie, *Just Enough Light for the Step I'm On: Trusting God in the Tough Times*, (Eugene, Oregon, Harvest House Publishers, 1999, 2008)

13   Wikipedia, *Bugs Bunny*, http://en.wikipedia.org/wiki/Bugs_Bunny.

14   Warren, Rick, *Purpose Driven Connection*, PurposeDriven. com, October 23, 2009.

15   Eldredge, John, *Walking with God*, (Nashville, Tennessee, Thomas Nelson, Inc., 2008) 198.

[16] Baker, John, *Life's Healing Choices*, (New York, NY, 2007) 44.

[17] Wiersbe, Warren, *Be Joyful*, (Colorado Springs, CO, 1974) 11.

[18] Bernardo, Rosemarie, *Aiea Woman is Excited for Her Saint in Making*,   http://archives.starbulletin.com/2008/07/04/news/story03.html

[19] Baker, John, *Life's Healing Choices*, (New York, NY, 2007) 138.

[20] HOLY BIBLE, NEW INTERNATIONAL VERSION, Copyright 1973, 1978, 1984 by International Bible Society, 583.

[21] Wiersbe, Warren, *Be Joyful*, (Colorado Springs, CO, 1974) 112.

Check out the *I Don't Buy Green Bananas* companion video (gbcompanion) at youtube.com URL Address: http://www.youtube.com/watch?v=sTwYAW4oHGA

CPSIA information can be obtained at www.ICGtesting.com
Printed in the USA
BVOW010534231012

303646BV00003B/5/P